Editors' Preface to Macmillan Stu... ...nomics

The rapid growth of academic literature in the field of economics has posed serious problems for both students and teachers of the subject. The latter find it difficult to keep pace with more than a few areas of their subject, so that an inevitable trend towards specialism emerges. The student quickly loses perspective as the maze of theories and models grows and the discipline accommodates an increasing amount of quantitative techniques.

'Macmillan Studies in Economics' is a new series which sets out to provide the student with short, reasonably critical surveys of the developments within the various specialist areas of theoretical and applied economics. At the same time, the studies aim to form an integrated series so that, seen as a whole, they supply a balanced overview of the subject of economics. The emphasis in each study is upon recent work, but each topic will generally be placed in a historical context so that the reader may see the logical development of thought through time. Selected bibliographies are provided to guide readers to more extensive works. Each study aims at a brief treatment of the salient problems in order to avoid clouding the issues in detailed argument. Nonetheless, the texts are largely self-contained, and presume only that the student has some knowledge of elementary micro-economics and macro-economics.

Mathematical exposition has been adopted only where necessary. Some recent developments in economics are not readily comprehensible without some mathematics and statistics, and quantitative approaches also serve to shorten what would otherwise be lengthy and involved arguments. Where authors have found it necessary to introduce mathematical techniques, these techniques have been kept to a minimum. The emphasis is upon the economics, and not upon the quantitative methods. Later studies in the series will provide analyses of the links between quantitative methods, in particular econometrics, and economic analysis.

MACMILLAN STUDIES IN ECONOMICS

General Editors: D. C. ROWAN and G. R. FISHER
Executive Editor: D. W. PEARCE

Published

John Burton: WAGE INFLATION
Miles Fleming: MONETARY THEORY
C. J. Hawkins and D. W. Pearce: CAPITAL INVESTMENT APPRAISAL
C. J. Hawkins: THEORY OF THE FIRM
David F. Heathfield: PRODUCTION FUNCTIONS
Dudley Jackson: POVERTY
P. N. Junankar: INVESTMENT: THEORIES AND EVIDENCE
J. E. King: LABOUR ECONOMICS
J. A. Kregel: THE THEORY OF ECONOMIC GROWTH
George McKenzie: THE MONETARY THEORY OF INTERNATIONAL TRADE
S. K. Nath: A PERSPECTIVE OF WELFARE ECONOMICS
D. W. Pearce: COST-BENEFIT ANALYSIS
Maurice Peston: PUBLIC GOODS AND THE PUBLIC SECTOR
David Robertson: INTERNATIONAL TRADE POLICY
Charles K. Rowley: ANTITRUST AND ECONOMIC EFFICIENCY
C. H. Sharp: TRANSPORT ECONOMICS
G. K. Shaw: FISCAL POLICY
R. Shone: THE PURE THEORY OF INTERNATIONAL TRADE
Frank J. B. Stilwell: REGIONAL ECONOMIC POLICY
John Vaizey: THE ECONOMICS OF EDUCATION
Peter A. Victor: ECONOMICS OF POLLUTION
Grahame Walshe: INTERNATIONAL MONETARY REFORM
E. Roy Weintraub: GENERAL EQUILIBRIUM THEORY

Forthcoming

G. Denton: ECONOMICS OF INDICATIVE PLANNING
J. A. Kregel: THEORY OF CAPITAL
Richard Lecomber: ECONOMIC GROWTH AND ENVIRONMENTAL QUALITY
D. Mayston: THE IDEA OF SOCIAL CHOICE
Simon Mohan: RADICAL ECONOMICS
B. Morgan: MONETARISM AND KEYNESIANISM
Christopher Nash: PUBLIC v. PRIVATE TRANSPORT
A. Peaker: BRITISH ECONOMIC GROWTH SINCE 1945
F. Pennance: HOUSING ECONOMICS
Nicholas Rau: TRADE CYCLES – THEORY AND EVIDENCE
M. Stabler: AGRICULTURAL ECONOMICS
E. Roy Weintraub: THE ECONOMICS OF CONFLICT AND CO-OPERATION
J. Wiseman: PRICING PROBLEMS OF THE NATIONALISED INDUSTRIES

The Monetary Theory of International Trade

GEORGE McKENZIE

Lecturer in Economics, University of Southampton

Macmillan

First published 1974 by
THE MACMILLAN PRESS LTD
London and Basingstoke
Associated companies in New York Dublin
Melbourne Johannesburg and Madras

SBN 333 12707 2

Printed in Great Britain by
THE ANCHOR PRESS LTD
Tiptree, Essex

Contents

Preface and Acknowledgements

This book represents extracts from lecture notes developed over the past seven years and delivered to students at Washington University, St Louis from 1966 to 1970 and at the University of Southampton over the past three years. Because of space considerations, I have been faced with the task of deciding which topics to include and which to exclude. From past experience I have found that it is best to develop a few subjects in some depth rather than to provide a cursory summary of a large, often complex body of knowledge. This is the approach adopted here. The book is thus not a complete survey of international monetary theory, although readers will find references to more than eighty relevant books and articles.

I would like to express my gratitude for the detailed comments provided by David Rowan and David Pearce of the University of Southampton, and by Ronald Shone of the University of Sheffield. Several Southampton students also offered helpful criticisms. I would also like to thank Mrs Jennie Burrow for typing the manuscript with speed and accuracy. Any omissions, inaccuracies or obscurities that remain are entirely my responsibility.

G. M.

1 Introduction

The purpose of this volume is to examine critically the literature dealing with balance of payments adjustments theories. As Krueger [43] has recently pointed out, there is no theory of international monetary economics. Economists have been unable to construct a simple general theory which can be refined and applied to a wide variety of problems. Instead we have a number of approaches to the theory of international adjustment. For example some models place great emphasis on the role that relative price changes may play whereas others concentrate on changes in output, inventories and/or employment that may arise when prices remain constant. Some models place great emphasis on the role that 'monetary' variables, such as the money supply or international capital flows, may play in the adjustment process, whilst other models concentrate on 'real' variables such as production, consumption and relative prices. To trace the developments that have occurred over the past twenty-five years, the reader may wish to consult the interesting surveys by Metzler [56], Haberler [22], Corden [12] and Krueger [43].

Our focal point here is the foreign exchange market and its operation under a number of assumptions about international monetary institutions. We shall examine the possible effects of a devaluation under the current 'adjustable peg' system. We shall also be concerned with how 'automatic' systems based on flexible exchange rates or the gold standard operate, in principle, to bring about equilibrium in the foreign exchange market. While alternative exchange-rate policies will receive much of our attention, the effects of discretionary monetary, fiscal and trade policies must also be considered important.

A major aim of this volume is to explain why the world economy, left to operate free of government intervention may not be capable of bringing about balance-of-payments equilibrium, full-employment or other desired goals. We shall also be concerned with the difficulties the authorities may face in achieving these aims.

The basic problem is that no one, producers, consumers, financial specialists or the authorities has complete, perfect information. No individual knows all the prices, quantities or level of government activity that will ensure that all markets will clear or that all social goals will be met. There is uncertainty. People base their decisions on expectations about future events, expectations about what other economic units are going to do. As a result mistakes will be made by both the private sector and the authorities. The important thing is to determine why errors are made and how people try to correct them. Thus in our discussions of various theoretical models and economic institutions, actual or proposed, we shall spend a good deal of time examining the assumptions about how various economic units take their decisions over time.

Unfortunately in dealing with these issues we can do no more than scratch the surface. The operation of the foreign exchange market and its interaction with other markets is complex. It is simply impossible for the human mind to disentangle *all* the relationships which may operate. As a result, to achieve even a *partial* understanding, the economist relies on relatively simple models to trace out the relationship between a few important variables that he is interested in. This procedure can be likened to an intellectual experiment. Physical scientists can study the relationship between a few variables by keeping all others constant within a laboratory. The economist obviously cannot treat the world as a laboratory and experiment with it. But he can perform some experiments abstractly.

Out of this research he may be able to further his understanding of the problems which are faced in the real world. However, as the model being used becomes more and more complex, it becomes more and more difficult to extract any information at all without quantitative information about the various parameters involved. Faced with this dilemma, some economists have been willing to overlook the partial nature of

10

the models with which they are dealing and have attempted to draw from them sweeping policy conclusions. From a logical point of view this approach is bound to be fraught with errors. One cannot hope to obtain accurate information from a model, the assumptions of which do not hold even approximately. For further thoughts on this, the reader is referred to Nagel [65].

However, there is another approach, one which would necessarily involve a reorientation of our research efforts. This shift of emphasis should be away from the construction of complicated models based on simple assumptions but which have limited policy conclusions. Instead more attention should be paid to understanding how various economic units, consumers, producers, banks, foreign exchange dealers, etc., take decisions about prices and quantities. Attention should then be paid to formulating behavioural relationships which can be tested and ultimately used to approximate forecasts about future economic activity.

In other words, international economists should be involved in two types of activities. One deals with the formulation of simple models with the aim of discovering useful but limited insights into actual problems. The other deals with the construction of models based on statistical methods which can provide us with an approximate mirror image of the real world.

2 Basic Assumptions and Relationships

In comparing the various approaches which have been developed in the literature, it will be important to determine whether the underlying model is *short run* or *long run*.

Within a short-run model the economist examines the impact of a particular event on certain variables which he believes are going to respond immediately. Other variables that may ultimately be affected, but only after a period of time, are assumed to remain constant. The analysis must therefore be considered as partial. The various economic units, e.g. consumers and producers, can be considered to be in a *state of equilibrium* since they have chosen the most desirable opportunities available to them within the time span under consideration. But if certain variables can be altered over a longer time span, it is clear that this partial, short-run equilibrium situation may be different from what consumers and producers may choose to do over the long run. We must therefore be aware that the ultimate, long-run impact of any policy may, and probably will be, different from that derived from our short-run partial theories.

On the other hand, short-run models do have an important role to play. For one thing, they enable us to perform the sort of intellectual experiments mentioned in the introductory chapter. The distinction between short run and long run can be a procedure for simplifying the framework of analysis so that only a few variables are actually studied. However, the short-run model has also had tremendous practical importance. Policy makers are certainly interested in the impact effects that an exchange rate variation or change in tariff policy may have not only on the balance of payments but on output and employment. This is basically the approach of 'Keynesian' economics – to design policies to deal with short-run problems.

Our characterisation of the short run has so far been rather general. How is the short run actually defined? What variables change and which are assumed constant? The answer is not clearcut since there are basically two concepts which dominate the literature. One relies on adjustments in prices to assure that market demand and supply are equal. The other assumes that this equality is assured by inventory adjustments. For further discussion, the reader is referred to Hicks [27] and Bushaw and Clower [5].

THE PRICE ADJUSTMENT MECHANISM

Let us suppose that producers of commodity X increase the quantity of output that they are willing to produce at any given price. The excess supply leads to a reduction in price. However, other markets will be affected. If other goods are substitutes for X, consumers will purchase less of the other commodities. The excess supply in these other markets will be eliminated, in turn, by the appropriate price reductions. For the price mechanism to operate in this fashion, we must assume that all economic units possess *complete information* about equilibrium prices and quantities in *all* markets. To allow for any errors means that one or more markets may not clear, that there will be an inventory change and consequently that the price mechanism has not brought about complete adjustment.

THE INVENTORY ADJUSTMENT MECHANISM

Under this scheme, it is explicitly assumed that prices remain constant. Any excess supply (demand) leads to an increase (decrease) in inventories held in the economy. This could take either of two forms. Either the excess supply will lead to an accumulation of inventories of the commodity under study, or to a reduction of output and hence to a reduction in the labour force employed. Which strategy is actually followed depends on the cost of holding commodity inventories (storage charges, interest fees, losses due to wastage, etc.) relative to the cost of discharging workers and then having to hire them back at some future time.

A crucial distinction between these two adjustment mechanisms is the formation of expectations about future prices and quantities. In the price-adjustment scheme it is assumed that expected prices coincide with actual prices. Otherwise there would be further adjustments. This is simply another way of saying that economic units act as if they possess complete information. In contrast the inventory adjustment mechanism assumes that people do not expect prices to change. Rather the view is that any increase (or decrease) in inventories will in the future be eliminated at current prices.

As described the inventory adjustment mechanisms is a short-run adjustment process. It recognises that individuals do not possess complete information and that they may make errors. In the long run, of course, the appropriate price and wage adjustments may be forthcoming as consumers, workers and business recognise that their expectations may have been wrong.

THE BASIC MODEL

Now let us turn to some of the specific assumptions which form the basis for our simple balance-of-payments adjustment theory. Here the emphasis will be on the interaction between imports and exports, the foreign exchange market and real domestic economic activity. In such analyses other possible international transactions (e.g. investment in foreign assets) are assumed to be given or are non-existent. For the sake of simplicity, let us also adopt the following assumptions:

1. There are only two countries in the world, say the United States and the United Kingdom. The citizens of each country consume only two commodities, cloth, which is produced only in Britain and wine, which is produced only in the U.S.A.

2. The citizens within each country have identical prefer-

ences and incomes although the preferences and income levels of British and Americans may differ. This assumption enables us to apply the theory of individual consumer behaviour to describe the overall community behaviour of an economy.

3. The only possible international transactions between private individuals involve Britain's exportable commodity, cloth, and the United States' exportable commodity, wine. There is no investment in the assets of one country by the citizens of the other. Indeed, there is no saving – all output is consumed.

4. The production of both commodities is quite rudimentary. It is assumed that the amount of labour employed is proportional to the level of output in each country. The volume of output is thus constrained by the size of its work force, which we assume to be constant. Labour is immobile between countries.

5. There is only one form of money, or medium of exchange, used in each country: gold pounds in the United Kingdom and gold dollars in the United States. Pounds can be exchanged for dollars via the foreign exchange market. What happens when there is excess demand or supply in this market depends largely upon the attitudes of the monetary authorities in each country. The various possibilities will be discussed in detail as we proceed.

6. If the value of a country's imports is greater than the value of its exports, we shall refer to that country as being in international payments deficit. Conversely, if the value of exports is greater than the value of imports, then the country is in surplus. (In later chapters, when we allow for international transactions in financial items, this definition must be modified.)

7. We shall initially assume that the foreign exchange dealers who act as intermediaries between buyers and sellers, do not hold any foreign exchange for their own account. Their sole function is to bring together buyer and seller at a mutually acceptable exchange rate. For doing this, they earn a commission.

3 The International Trade Offer Curve

The demand for foreign exchange is a derived demand depending on a country's demand for products manufactured abroad. Conversely the supply of foreign exchange depends on foreign demand for the home country's produce. Thus in order to understand how the foreign exchange market operates, we must examine the factors determining a country's trading patterns. In doing so we shall build a formal model based upon the assumptions listed in Chapter 2. Of particular importance is an analytical tool called an offer curve. This device was first applied to international economic problems by Mill [59] but was considerably improved by Marshall [51]. Up-to-date treatments appear in Meade [54] and Pearce [69]. In order to construct this device we must review the basic elements of the theory of consumer behaviour.

Let us denote the price of cloth and wine in the United Kingdom by p_c and p_w, respectively. Similarly q_c and q_w represent the price of the goods in the United States. If e represents the exchange rate and is expressed as the number of dollars per pound (the way it appears in both British and American financial newspapers), then

$$q_c = e \cdot p_c$$
$$q_w = e \cdot p_w$$

Thus the relative price ratio in the United Kingdom can be written as

$$\frac{p_w}{p_c} = \frac{1}{e} \cdot \frac{q_w}{p_c}$$

If the prices of the two goods are constant in their *country of origin*, relative prices can change if the exchange rate is allowed to vary. For example if e rises such that the British find it cheaper to obtain dollars, then the price of wine in Britain will fall relative to the price of cloth. An increase in e is equivalent to a devaluation from the American point of view and an upward-revaluation from the British viewpoint. Relative prices in the United Kingdom may also vary as a result of an

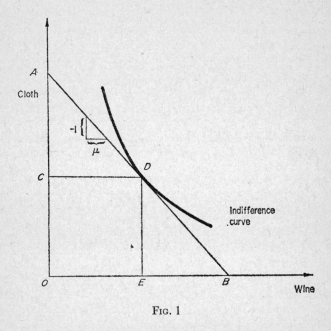

Fig. 1

excess supply or demand for one or both commodities, in which case p_w and p_c may change even though the exchange rate is fixed.

In considering Fig. 1 we assume that the theory of individual consumer behaviour can be used to describe the behaviour of a community. A sufficient condition for this to be the case is that all consumers possess identical preferences. Suppose that the line AB represents the budget constraint faced by the citizens of the United Kingdom and that OA represents the maximum output that is possible, given the supply of labour

18

in Britain. Since workers are the only inputs into the production process, the proceeds from the sale of OA will represent their income. As consumers, they could spend all of that income on OA units of cloth or all of their income on OB units of wine. Or the British consumers could buy some combination of the two commodities along AB, say OC units of cloth and OE units of wine. OC would therefore represent domestic consumption of cloth in Britain, AC British exports of cloth and OE its imports of wine. Any such combination of purchases will completely exhaust consumers' income.

The slope of the line AB is equal to the price ratio p_w/p_c. To see this, suppose that one less unit of cloth were purchased. This leaves one unit of cloth times p_c available to be spent on μ units of wine, i.e.

$$1 \times p_c = \mu \times p_w$$

Rearranging this relationship and referring again to Fig. 1, we note[1]

$$\text{slope of budget line } AB = \frac{1}{\mu} = \frac{p_w}{p_c}$$

This ratio indicates the 'terms of trade'.[1]

The assumption is made that consumers will always choose that combination of commodities which maximises their satisfaction, given prices and incomes. If D represents such a combination, then at that point there will be a community indifference curve tangent to the budget constraint. This indicates that no higher indifference curve is feasible. Any move away from D will make consumers less happy.

EXPENDITURE SWITCHING EFFECTS

Consider Fig. 2. Suppose that there is an increase in the price of wine. This means that British consumers now face a steeper price line AF and as a result choose the commodity bundle represented by K. A fall in the price of wine could result in the budget line AG, with the commodity bundle at J being

[1] For simplicity, we are neglecting the negative sign of the slope.

19

consumed. If we allow the price of wine to vary from infinity on down, we will trace out the 'price-consumption' line *AM* indicating the various combinations of goods that consumers will purchase at the different prices.

While the curve *AM* is most frequently referred to as a 'price-consumption' line, given the assumptions of our model, it can also play the role of Britain's international trade *offer curve*. We noted that at the price ratio, indicated by the slope of *AB*, Britain consumed *OC* of its own exportable commodity

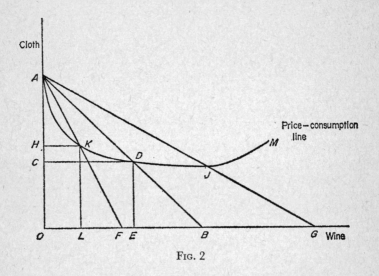

Fig. 2

while it imported *OE* of the U.S. exportable. Since full employment output is assumed constant at *OA*, this situation leaves *AC* units of cloth available for export. In other words, Britain is willing to offer *AC* units of cloth for *OE* units of wine. A similar argument can be made with respect to all the other points along *AM*.

The shape of the offer curve has some important implications as we shall shortly see. It should be noted that as we move along the offer curve from *A* to *J* purchases of cloth decline while the consumption of wine increases. Over this range the price of wine has fallen relative to the price of cloth. When the offer curve yields these results, the two goods are said to be

20

gross substitutes: i.e. as the price of wine falls relative to the price of cloth buyers substitute wine for cloth.

As we move along the offer curve beyond J and toward M the situation is different even though the price of wine continues to fall relative to the price of cloth. Here the consumption of both goods increases; as a result, over this range, the commodities are classified as *gross complements*. The commodities need not reverse their characteristics in this fashion. Indeed the offer curve might be drawn in such a way that both goods are always considered substitutes or, alternatively, always complementary.

EXPENDITURE CHANGING EFFECTS

The preceding analysis assumed that total expenditure remained constant as relative prices were varied. In this section we shall determine what happens when total expenditure varies but prices and the exchange rate remain constant. Changes in expenditure can be brought about through a variety of governmental actions: (1) changes in the level of spending by the authorities either on goods or on direct payments to individuals; (2) changes in the level of taxation; (3) changes in monetary policy which affect expenditure through alterations in interest rates and the money supply.

Let us begin again with the budget line AB and the commodity bundle D. In Fig. 3 if expenditure increases a new combination of goods will be chosen, e.g. the combination at T. If expenditure fell, the bundle at S might be chosen. If we identify the combinations of goods chosen at various levels of expenditure, it is possible to construct an 'income-consumption' line such as OV. Under these circumstances both goods can be classified as *normal*, since consumers buy more of both when expenditure increases, and conversely. On the other hand, if the income-consumption line was represented by the dotted line, cloth would be classified as an *inferior* good since less of it is bought as expenditure rises. Wine is still treated as normal, however.

Some implications, useful for later discussions, can be drawn. First, provided both goods are normal, as expenditure increases,

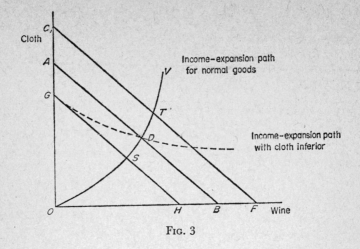

FIG. 3

so will the import of wine and consumption of home-produced cloth. This means that out of current output, less cloth is available for export from Britain. In the short run, of course,

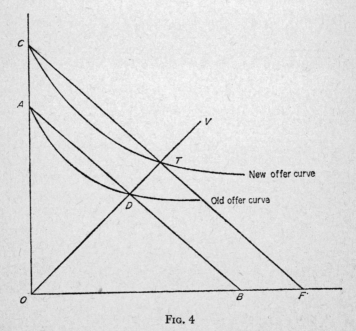

FIG. 4

any demands in excess of full-employment supply *OA* could be met out of inventories. Second, as expenditure changes there will be a shift in the offer curve, as in Fig. 4 where such a shift occurs because of an increase in expenditure. It should be noted that the offer curves intersect the income-expansion path and the budget constraint at the same point, e.g. *D* or *T*. This is because there are indifference curves tangent to the budget constraints at *D* and *T* respectively. That is, consumers are maximising their satisfaction at the prices and expenditure associated with those bundles of cloth and wine.

4 Price Adjustments and Flexible Exchange Rates

Prior to the appearance of Keynes' *General Theory* [40] in 1936 and, indeed, until the late 1940s, balance-of-payments adjustment theory was primarily concerned with the analysis of mechanisms that would automatically restore equilibrium in the foreign exchange market. Cf. Metzler [56]. It was assumed that the price mechanism operated in such a smooth fashion that not only this equilibrium but also full-employment would be achieved. Two alternative systems were explored: flexible exchange rates and the gold standard. While both depended upon market prices to adjust speedily, the emphasis was different. In the former the exchange rate bore the burden of adjustment, whereas under the gold standard, commodity prices would indirectly be affected through automatic variations in the money supply.

In either case, relative prices would have to change in such a fashion that any disequilibrium in the foreign exchange market is eliminated. For example, in the case where British demand for dollars was greater than the supply, it was hoped that prices would change in such a way as to switch spending from U.S. goods to British products.

In order to determine the outcome of such adjustments, it is necessary to learn how the offer curves for both the United Kingdom and the United States relate to one another. This is accomplished through the use of the so-called Edgeworth–Bowley box diagram. We shall then examine the operation of a flexible exchange rate system, postponing until the next chapter a discussion of the gold standard.

In Fig. 5(a) we depict the U.K. offer curve as drawn in Fig. 1 under the assumption that the output of cloth involves the full-employment of available labour. In a similar manner we

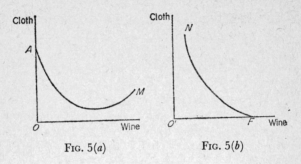

FIG. 5(a)   FIG. 5(b)

construct the offer curve for the United States in Fig. 5(b). We extend it from point F since this represents the full-employment level of wine output in the United States. If we now

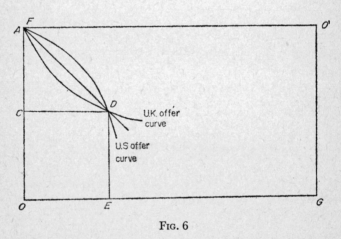

FIG. 6

invert Fig. 5(b) and place it on top of diagram 5(a) so that points A and F coincide, we obtain the famous box diagram, Fig. 6.

The situation depicted here represents a full, long-run equilibrium for our simple model. First, note that in this case there is only one possible combination of goods for which the offers made by the two countries will coincide, the combinations at D. At this point, with the terms of trade indicated by the slope of AD, the United Kingdom will want to export AC units of cloth for OE units of wine. Correspondingly, America will want to export OE units of wine for AC units of cloth.

Not only do the offers coincide, but the total demand for both products is equal to the full-employment output in the two countries. This can easily be seen by noting that U.K. citizens consume OC units of cloth and OE units of wine, while U.S. citizens consume AC units of cloth and EG units of wine. Full-employment output in the United Kingdom is OA and equals OC plus AC. Similarly, in the U.S.A., full-employment output OG equals OE plus EG.

A further outcome of this exercise is that the foreign exchange market is also in equilibrium: the value of U.K. exports equals the value of U.K. imports, i.e. the balance of trade is equal to zero. This can be seen as follows. The slope of AD equals

$$- \frac{\text{price of wine}}{\text{price of cloth}} = - \frac{p_w}{p_c}$$

It also equals

$$- AC/OE$$

Therefore

$$\frac{AC}{OE} = \frac{p_w}{p_c}$$

or $p_c AC = p_w OE$ where $p_c AC$ is the value of cloth exports and $p_w OE$ the value of wine imports.

BALANCE-OF-TRADE DISEQUILIBRIUM

Suppose, however, that the situation depicted in Fig. 7 existed. At the terms of trade indicated by the slope of AS, there is deficient demand for cloth since:

O'L plus *OH* is less than *OA*, the full-employment output of cloth in the United Kingdom

and excess demand for wine since:

OJ plus *O'K* is greater than *OG*, the full-employment output of wine in the United States

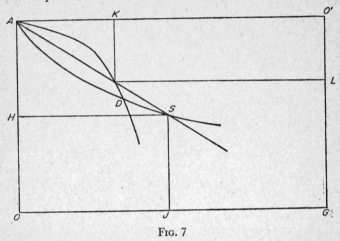

Fig. 7

Further, there is a disequilibrium in the foreign exchange market. This can be seen by noting that the value of U.K. exports *O'L* is equivalent in value to *AK* units of wine. But this quantity is less than the actual amount of imports *OJ*. There is thus an excess demand for dollars. The dollars generated from exports are less than those desired for imports.

The above situation can also be characterised in another way which will be useful in later discussions. Expressed in terms of cloth, total U.K. expenditure equals *OH*, the consumption of domestically produced output, plus *AH*, the value of imports. Total sales, *Y*, equals *OH* plus *O'L*, the amount of cloth exported. Thus:[1]

$$Y \equiv OH + O'L$$
$$\equiv OH + AH + O'L - AH$$
$$\equiv A + B$$

[1] The symbol $\equiv$ indicates that the relationship is an identity. The equal sign $=$ indicates that the relationship is a structural or behavioural equation.

28

where A is total expenditure, $OH+AH$ (labelled *absorption* by Alexander [2]) and B is the balance of trade, $O'L-AH$. That is to say if absorption is less than the value of output the United Kingdom has a trade surplus, and if absorption is greater than the value of output, she has a trade deficit.

Let us suppose that the home price of each exportable commodity remains constant, i.e. in the short run prices do not respond to the pressures of excess demand or supply. Exchange rates can vary, however. Given the situation depicted in Fig. 7, foreign exchange dealers will find that the demand for dollars exceeds the amount being supplied at the existing exchange rate indicated by the slope of AS. If we assume that dealers do not hold any foreign exchanges balances, they will eliminate the excess demand for dollars by lowering the price of pounds in terms of dollars. As a result, the terms of trade line AS will become steeper until the disequilibrium in the foreign exchange market is eliminated, the situation at D.

CONDITIONS FOR INSTABILITY

The above discussion assumed that the world was 'stable'. That is, an excess of supply over demand for dollars causes the price of dollars in terms of pounds to fall. Conversely, an excess of demand over supply causes the price of dollars in terms of pounds to rise. However, it is possible that an existing equilibrium may be 'unstable' according to the above definition.

Consider Fig. 8, where points A, B and C each represent an equilibrium situation with demand equal to supply in all markets. However, point B is an unstable equilibrium. A slight increase in the exchange rate will send the terms of trade line away from B in the direction of C; a slight decrease in the rate will send the terms of trade line toward A. For example, at the terms of trade indicated by the line JD, there is excess demand for cloth and excess supply of wine. U.K. exports are thus greater than its imports and as a result the supply of dollars to the foreign exchange market is greater than its imports, and as a result the supply of dollars to the

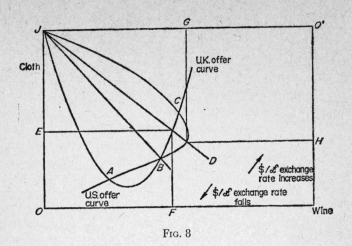

FIG. 8

foreign exchange market is greater than the demand. The terms of trade line will become flatter, moving the two economies toward C. The reader can check for himself the implications of a terms of trade line steeper than JB. In this case equilibrium will be restored at A. It is clear that B is 'unstable' in the sense that a disturbance from it will not set in motion forces returning the world economy to it.

The existence of an unstable equilibrium has some rather important implications. In the situation depicted in Fig. 7, as well as the situations associated with points A or C in Fig. 8, an excess demand for dollars leads to a depreciation of the pound whereas an excess supply leads to an appreciation. These are results which intuitively we would expect to hold. However, around B an excess demand for dollars leads to an appreciation whereas an excess supply leads to a depreciation.

It is therefore of some interest to identify conditions under which a flexible exchange rate system will be stable in the above sense. There are two possible approaches.

1. A *sufficient* condition for stability is that both commodities be gross substitutes in each country. This guarantees the situation depicted in Fig. 7. It rules out the possibility of the offer curves turning back so as to produce the situation in Fig. 8. This condition can be attributed to Marshall [51].

2. A *necessary and sufficient* condition is that the sum of the

elasticities of demand for importables by the two countries sum to less than minus one. This is due to Bickerdike [4]. However, it has become known as the *Marshall–Lerner condition*. This terminology is indeed odd. For one thing, Marshall's condition, noted above, bears little resemblance to this one. Secondly, although Lerner [45] does derive this formula, he is concerned with whether a devaluation under a fixed exchange rate system will improve the balance of trade or not. This is an entirely different problem from determining whether a flexible exchange rate system is stable or not. At this point it should be emphasised that much of the literature on stability analysis is in terms of elasticities of demand for 'imports' rather than 'importables'. Since there may be some home production, the two in general, will be different. For further discussion, see Chapter 7.

As Mundell [63] has pointed out, stability in the above sense is not deduced from a truly dynamic model. It is timeless. Although Mundell seeks to justify this approach on heuristic grounds, from the point of view of understanding actual exchange rate movements, we need to know more about actual decision-making processes. While it is indeed true that it is difficult to derive clearcut results from more complex models without knowledge of the various parameters involved, this should be a call for more empirical research rather than a retreat to simple models which yield results but the assumptions of which are patently unrealistic.

The above stability conditions require (*a*) that all related commodity and labour markets are in equilibrium and (*b*) that no trading takes place when the foreign exchange market is out of equilibrium. That is, it assumes that there exists an auctioneer who brings together all the foreign exchange dealers and then establishes exchange rates so as to match up all their requirements. If the markets did not clear in this fashion, exchange dealers would find that their inventories were varying.

The implications of this process are clear. All transactors must possess complete information about the combination of prices and quantities necessary to clear every market. In other words, expectations about variable changes must coincide

31

exactly with the actual changes necessary for equilibrium to be restored. If this does not occur, then the above analysis must be modified.

For example suppose that entrepreneurs do not vary current prices because they believe that they are the normal ones. In the short run, the situation in Fig. 8 will be maintained. It will appear as if there is no mechanism working to restore equilibrium. Of course, in the long run, U.K. businesses will be unwilling to let inventories pile up whereas U.S. businesses will soon find their stocks exhausted. But this process may take quite a while to work itself out.

In this discussion of 'price-adjustment' or 'inventory-adjustment' processes, we have assumed that there will be symmetric behaviour, irrespective of whether there is excess market demand or excess supply. However, there is good reason to believe that behaviour may be asymmetric. U.S. wine producers, facing growing demand, may increase their prices, so as to raise their profits, rather than let inventories fall. This also gives them a capital gain on their inventories which were produced to sell at a lower price. On the other hand the British cloth industry may decide neither to lower prices nor to let inventories rise, but instead to cut back output and employment. If workers believe that the current wage is the normal one, they may be unwilling to accept lower wages, but instead may decide to go without work for a while. They bear the burden of the adjustment.

Given these possibilities, it becomes quite clear that the analysis of the foregoing sections is indeed limited and that we need to know and incorporate into the analysis more information about adjustment processes – even if we confine the analysis to the short run.

5 Fixed Exchange Rates, The Gold Standard and The Quantity Theory of Money

The analysis of the previous chapter can easily be extended to the case of fixed exchange rates. Instead of relying on exchange variations to restore equilibrium in the foreign exchange market, this system depends upon commodity prices to restore equilibrium in the goods markets. Thus the situation depicted in Fig. 8 involves an excess supply of cloth and an excess demand for wine. The price for cloth will tend to fall while the price of wine tends to rise. The terms-of-trade line will become steeper thereby moving the economy toward equilibrium at D. However, as noted in the last chapter, this analysis does not explicitly take into account the characteristics of the adjustment process over time. This is particularly true for the above situation which requires that cloth manufacturers and wine producers, located in different countries must somehow co-ordinate their price and output decisions so as to bring about an equilibrium terms of trade.

On the other hand the gold-standard mechanism explicitly assumes a complex, but still inadequate, adjustment mechanism. The seeds for this idea appear in Hume [29] and their development is discussed in detail by Viner [82]. A recent rehabilitation has been attempted by Rueff [73].

A NAÏVE QUANTITY THEORY OF MONEY

As we assumed earlier each country possesses a certain number of gold coins (denominated in its own unit of exchange), which comprise its money supply.

During any specified period of time, say a year, this money supply will turn over a certain number of times. For example, over the period of a month, the business sector will receive the proceeds of its sales to home and foreign buyers. These proceeds represent the value of the money supply, and are paid out at the end of every month in the form of wages. In turn these funds are spent on home produced and imported goods. As we saw earlier, if the value of exports and imports are the same, then absorption is equal to the value of output. Every month, the money supply will pass from the hands of industry to consumers and back to industry, thus turning over twelve times during a year. This turnover rate will be referred to as the velocity of circulation, V. Thus the money supply multiplied by the velocity of circulation, in this case 12, will equal the value of output for the year. In other words

$$M \cdot V = P \cdot \overline{Q}$$

where P is the price level of the home produced good and T is the number of transactions over the year. $\overline{Q}$ represents full-employment output, a constant. This level can be maintained since workers are assumed to be willing to accept the sales proceeds as wages. The velocity of circulation is also a constant determined by the number of times wages are paid during a specific period. The result of these two conditions is that the price level varies directly with the supply of money. This is often referred to as the 'naïve' Quantity Theory of Money.

THE FULL-EMPLOYMENT ASSUMPTION

One of the basic assumptions underlying the theory of the gold-standard is that the economy is always in full-employment. Any adjustments that may occur in the balance of payments will take place so as to preserve this situation. In other words, the case described in Fig. 7, where there was excess supply of cloth and excess demand for wine, is ruled out. Rather we are restricted to analysing the type of situation depicted in Fig. 9.

In this diagram total demand for each commodity is equal

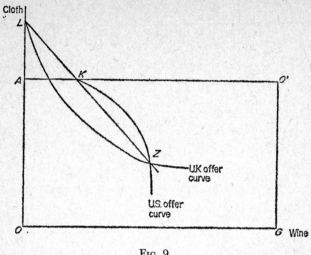

FIG. 9

to its full-employment output. However, aggregate spending in
the United Kingdom, OL in terms of cloth, is greater than
OA, the output of cloth. Thus Britain has a trade deficit.
Similarly aggregate spending in the United States is less
than output there: they have a trade surplus. As a result the
money supply (gold) falls in Britain and increases in America.
According to the naïve quantity theory, the price of cloth
falls whereas the price of wine rises. This has two implications.
First, it changes relative prices in such a way as to make
the terms of trade line LZ steeper. Second, as cash balances
fall in the United Kingdom and rise in the United States,
expenditure will decrease in the former and increase in the
latter. Thus not only will the terms of trade line become
steeper but it will be shifting to the left as well. Similarly the
two offer curves will be shifting, and in such a way that full-
employment is always maintained. The implication of this is
that the terms of trade line and offer curves must always
move in such a way that the intersection of the two curves
occurs on the terms of trade line, as in Fig. 9.

In Chapter 4 we noted that the adjustment process might
not operate in a symmetric fashion. This result also follows
from Keynes' restatement of the quantity theory: 'So long

as there is unemployment, *unemployment* will change in the same proportion as the quantity of money.' [40, p. 296].

The implications of this process for the gold-standard mechanism are as follows (provided, of course, that the demand for importables is reasonably elastic). As before the U.S. trade surplus leads to an increase in the U.S. money supply and then to an increase in the price of wine. In Britain, the trade deficit leads to a reduction in the money supply and a subsequent increase in unemployment – not a reduction in the price of cloth. The result is similar to that established at the end of Chapter 4. Just what trading pattern will be established in the short run cannot be ascertained without further information about the speeds with which the various interrelated markets adjust.

Further, as Friedman [18] has emphasised, the demand for money depends on a wide variety of variables, not just total income. These other variables include actual and expected interest rates, actual and expected rates of inflation, to name a few. For example, suppose that there is an increase in the money supply due to a payments surplus. If prices begin to rise, consumers expecting further increases may rush to buy now before those increases materialise. The increased money supply has a very potent impact on economic activity. On the other hand if consumers believe that any price increases are temporary, they will withold purchases in the hope that prices will fall. In this case the quantity theory would not appear to work, at least not in the short run.

Despite these difficulties, there is much to be learned by studying the implications of the gold-standard mechanism. In a classic paper, Johnson [37] developed Alexander's absorption approach [2], clarifying many issues and relating them to actual policy problems. He argued that a payments deficit meant either (a) that cash balances were falling at home and that ultimately through a gold-standard type of adjustment process, payments equilibrium would be restored or (b) that the authorities were somehow neutralising or offsetting the dishoarding. For example in our simple model where gold is the sole medium of exchange, the authorities could buy goods with stocks of gold held by them but not in circulation. In actual practice, the dishoarding can be neutralised by open market operations. This possibility is discussed in Chapter 8.

A second important aspect of Johnson's paper was his attempt to characterise the decision processes leading up to a situation where payments were different from receipts. Utilising the terminology developed by Bushaw and Clower [5], Johnson distinguished between a 'stock' deficit and a 'flow' deficit. In the first case payments and receipts may differ as individuals attempt to reallocate their holdings of goods and securities. When equilibrium stocks are achieved, transactors no longer have any reason for maintaining payments different from receipts. Equality between the two will be restored and hence any payments deficit or surplus will be eliminated.

A flow deficit on the other hand may emerge as a result of a change in relative prices. If the automatic adjustment mechanism, referred to above, is allowed to work itself out, then this deficit will also be temporary. However, such a situation requires that the authorities follow a conscious policy of allowing cash balances to fall. If they maintain the money supply constant, then the deficit will persist. Johnson also discussed the impact of 'expenditure-changing' and 'expenditure-switching' policies. The argument here has already been discussed in Chapters 3 and 4, to which the reader is referred.

6 International Trade Multipliers

In the 1920s and 1930s, Frank Taussig [78] and a number of his students investigated the operation of the gold standard to determine if it worked according to the existing theory. Although prices and gold flows tended to move in the expected direction, the 'surprising exactness and speed' with which the adjustments occurred tended to create doubts in Taussig's mind. Relatively small gold flows and relative price changes seemed to be able to restore equilibrium in the balance of payments with remarkable ease.

The missing link followed the publication of Keynes' *General Theory* [40], and involved the generalisation of a simple macro-economic model to the case when two or more nations were trading with each other. As we shall demonstrate below, this framework yields two important results. First, changes in income and employment, without price variations, will tend to bring about partial adjustment in a country's balance of payments. Second, international trade is a powerful vehicle for the propagation of business cycles internationally. Two basic references on this topic are Machlup [46] and Johnson [34].

Let us assume that each country is operating at less than full-employment and that prices remain constant. The economies of each country can be described by the following relationships:

$$D_1 = a_1 Y_1 \quad (6.1a) \qquad D_2 = a_2 Y_2 \quad (6.1b)$$
$$M_1 = b_1 Y_1 \quad (6.2b) \qquad M_2 = b_2 Y_2 \quad (6.2b)$$
$$X_1 \equiv M_2 \quad (6.3c) \qquad X_2 \equiv M_1 \quad (6.3b)$$
$$Y_1 \equiv D_1 + X_1 + G_1 \quad (6.4d) \qquad Y_2 \equiv D_2 + X_2 + G_2 \quad (6.4b)$$

where D_i represents i's consumption of its own output

M_i the value of i's imports

X_i the value of i's exports

G_i exogenous expenditure in i (e.g. autonomous investment, government spending, etc.)

Y_i the value of i's national output

a_i country i's propensity to consume its own output out of income

b_i country i's propensity to import

Equations (6.1) and (6.2) indicate that consumption in both countries of home produced goods and imports depends only on income. Equation (6.3) simply indicates that in a two-country world one's imports must equal two's exports, and conversely. Equation (6.4) is the national income identity.

We are now in a position to determine the effect that a change in one of the exogenous variables G_1 or G_2 may have on the level of income in both countries.[1] First, let us substitute (6.1) – (6.3) into (6.4) to obtain

$$Y_1 = a_1 Y_1 + b_2 Y_2 + G_1 \qquad (6.5a)$$
$$Y_2 = a_2 Y_2 + b_1 Y_1 + G_2 \qquad (6.5b)$$

We have two equations which can readily be solved for Y_1 and Y_2 as follows[2]

$$Y_1 = \frac{1}{D}\{(1-a_2)G_1 + b_2 G_2\} \qquad (6.6a)$$

$$Y_2 = \frac{1}{D}\{b_1 G_1 + (1-a_1)G_2\} \qquad (6.6b)$$

where $\qquad D = (1-a_1)(1-a_2) - b_1 b_2$

[1] We are here comparing two different short-run equilibrium situations in which the level of unplanned expenditure is zero.

[2] Rewrite 6.5 as:

$$(1-a_1)Y_1 - b_2 Y_2 = G_1$$
$$-b_1 Y_1 + (1-a_2)Y_2 = G_2$$

Then multiply the first equation by b_1 and the second by $(1-a_1)$. Add the two equations to obtain (6.6b). Now start again. Multiply the first equation by $(1-a_2)$ and the second by b_2. Add the equations to obtain (6.6a).

It is now clear that an increase in G_1 is going to have an effect on the level of income in both Y_1 and Y_2. The multipliers are $(1-a_2)/D$ and b_1/D respectively. Since b_1 and a_2 are both positive and less than one, the numerators will be positive. Determining the sign of D is more complicated, however. Let us assume that each country does not spend all of its income on commodities but saves or hoards a certain proportion, s_1 and s_2 respectively. Therefore

$$a_1 + b_1 + s_1 \equiv 1$$
$$a_2 + b_2 + s_2 \equiv 1$$

By substituting these two equations into the expression for D we obtain

$$D = (b_1 + s_1)(b_2 + s_2) - b_1 b_2$$
$$= b_1 s_2 + b_2 s_1 + s_1 s_2$$

which is clearly positive. Thus all the multipliers will be positive. While the absolute magnitude of the multipliers depends on the sizes of the various parameters, it is possible to compare their relative sizes. An increase in exogenous expenditure in country one, G_1, will have a greater impact on national income there Y_1 than an increase in G_2 which is equal to G_1. The reason for this is an increase in G_1 immediately increases Y_1. G_2 increases Y_2 immediately and only a fraction of that will lead to increased exports and additional income for country one.

Let us now examine the impact that changes in G_1 and G_2 will have on the balance of trade, B equal to $X_1 - M_1$. Utilising (6.2) and (6.6) we obtain:

$$B = \frac{b_2}{D}\{b_1 G_1 + (1-a_1)G_2\} - \frac{b_1}{D}\{(1-a_2)G_1 + b_2 G_2\} \quad (6.9)$$

which reduces to

$$B = \frac{b_1 s_2}{D} G_1 + \frac{b_2 s_1}{D} G_2 \quad (6.7)$$

Thus an increase in G_1 worsens one's trade balance (and improves two's) whereas an increase in G_2 improves one's trade balance (and worsens two's).

International trade multipliers are a powerful tool for explaining the transmission of business cycles between countries. For contrast, let us compare the above multipliers with those based on the assumption that Britain or the United States is very small. That is, any changes in the small country's imports does not have any significant effect on spending in the rest of the world. This comparison will enable us to see whether the transmission mechanism dampens or amplifies the effect of any exogenous change.

Substitute (6.1a) into (6.3a) to yield

$$Y_1 = a_1 Y_1 + X_1 + G_1$$

Therefore

$$Y_1 = \frac{1}{1-a_1} X_1 + \frac{1}{1-a_1} G_1$$

Here the exogenous spending multiplier is $1/(1-a_1)$ compared with $(1-a_2)/D$ the multiplier for G_1 in our multi-country model. We can rewrite this latter expression, dividing both numerator and denominator by $(1-a_2)$, as:

$$\frac{1}{(1-a_1) - \{b_1 b_2/(1-a_2)\}}$$

It is easy to see that when feedback effects from other countries are allowed the multiplier is greater than when they are not. Thus the feedback effects tend to amplify the original exogenous change.

A comparison of trade balance multipliers is also possible. For the small country unaffected by the feedbacks

$$B = X_1 - b_1 \left\{ \frac{1}{1-a_1} X_1 + \frac{1}{1-a_1} G_1 \right\}$$

This is obtained from equations (6.2) and (6.6). The multiplier for G_1 is $-b_1/(1-a_1)$. We can rewrite the relevant multiplier for G_1 in equation (6.7) as

$$-\frac{b_1 s_2}{D} = -\frac{b_1}{1-a_1} \left\{ \frac{s_2(1-a_1)}{(1-a_1)(1-a_2) - b_1 b_2} \right\}$$

$$= -\frac{b_1}{1-a_1} \left(\frac{b_1 s_2 + s_1 s_2}{b_1 s_2 + b_2 s_1 + s_1 s_2} \right)$$

42

Since the term in brackets is less than one, the multi-country multiplier is less than the small-country multiplier. The implication is that the secondary feedback effects tend to dampen the balance-of-payments impact of an exogenous variable change. However, the dampening is not complete.

The multiplier analysis developed here has been expanded in a number of ways by Chipman [10], Goodwin [21] and Airov [1]. Additional countries can be included; the possibility of lagged responses can be allowed for; and additional functional relationships, e.g. equations explaining investment behaviour, can be incorporated. Thus we can incorporate information about adjustment processes and hence trace out the variations of output and national trade balances over time.

There is one assumption implicit in this analysis which needs to be mentioned. We noted above that the income adjustment mechanism will not work to bring about complete balance-of-payments equilibrium. However, in earlier chapters we assumed that a deficit (surplus) would work to reduce (increase) cash balances and hence change expenditure in such a way as to restore equilibrium. Implicitly, multiplier analysis assumes that any such variations in domestic supplies are neutralised by the authorities. This possibility will be discussed in Chapter 9. For example, the authorities can neutralise the monetary effects of a trade deficit by buying securities on the open market; thus they restore the level of cash balances. Thus the use of multiplier analysis as stated in this chapter, implicitly assumes a particular type of reaction by the authorities.

7 Inventory Changes, Unemployment and Discretionary Adjustment Policies

Following the Second World War, economists came to place more and more emphasis on the implications of discretionary economic policies for balance-of-payments adjustment. Attention began to turn away from the role of automatic price adjustments through gold-standard or flexible exchange-rate systems to the role of monetary and fiscal policies and trade restrictions. The difficulties alluded to earlier, about the reliability of the price mechanism to achieve adjustment were increasingly recognised; that is, serious, undesirable dislocations might arise as that adjustment process worked itself out. It became clear that in the short run there could arise conflicts between policy objectives, e.g. between full-employment and balance-of-payments equilibrium. It is the purpose of this chapter to elaborate on some of the reasons why these difficulties may occur and to show how various 'policy packages' might work.

THE PROBLEM

Let us return to the problem raised in the previous chapter. There is deficient demand for U.K. cloth, excess demand for U.S. wine and a trade deficit (surplus) for the U.K. (U.S.). In other words, deflationary pressures are building up in

45

the United Kingdom whereas inflationary pressures exist in the United States. We will assume that prices do not adjust; rather, inventories fall in America whereas in Britain businesses contract output and the amount of labour employed.

For simplicity, we shall also assume that the U.S. authorities are rather passive and simply maintain total expenditure at AO' in Fig. 10. Exchange rates are fixed. Under these circumstances, Great Britain has a choice between (a) eliminating its trade deficit but incurring unemployment and (b) maintaining full-employment but causing a payments deficit. Let us now see why this is the case.

If Britain decides to eliminate its trade deficit, it can do so by lowering total expenditure from OA to OT. This shifts the U.K. offer curve so that it intersects the budget constraint TW vertically below the point where the U.S. offer curve intersects the U.S. budget constraint AZ. As a result, it will consume OR cloth and OS wine. In return for the wine it will export RT units of cloth. This is exactly equal to the offer that the United States will want to make: ON wine in return for AQ cloth. (AQ is equal to TR, since the triangle TAZ is the same size as the triangle RTW.) In addition to the achievement of equilibrium in the foreign exchange market, the excess demand for the U.S. product, wine, has been eliminated. Total demand, ON plus NG, equals total output OG. That is, the United States is producing at full-employment.

However, such is not the case in the United Kingdom. In order to achieve a payments equilibrium, output of cloth has now been reduced below the full-employment level OA. There is now an obvious conflict between maintaining a zero balance-of-trade and full-employment if the exchange rate is to be maintained. In order to examine the implications of this conflict in somewhat greater detail let us spell out further the relationship between the exchange rate and U.K. domestic expenditure policy if external balance is the goal.

We showed in Chapter 3 that the slope of the price line, e.g. AS in Fig. 10 is proportional to $1/e$ where e is in terms of dollars per pound. Provided that the offer curves are shaped as they are (i.e. the goods are gross substitutes), the flatter the price line the greater will the expenditure reduction be needed to achieve a zero trade balance. That is, in such circumstances, fewer pounds will be needed to purchase dollars, and as a result American goods appear relatively cheaper. The excess demand for wine and the excess supply of cloth are both greater. Hence, to achieve commodity market equilibrium the larger must be the reduction in expenditure. This relationship between the exchange rate, e, and total domestic U.K. expenditure, E, is traced out in Fig. 11. It is represented by the schedule labelled foreign exchange market equilibrium.

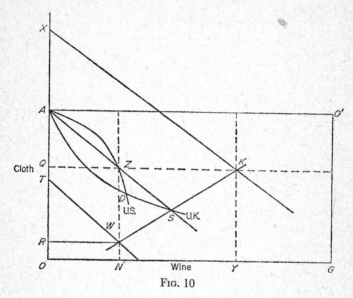

Fig. 10

Let us now suppose that Great Britain is concerned with achieving full-employment instead of external balance. If total expenditure is increased from OA to OX, the U.K. offer curve shifts so that it intersects the U.K. budget constraint at K. Total demand for cloth, OQ by the United Kingdom and AQ by the United States now equals the full-employment supply of cloth. However, both the foreign exchange market and market for wine in the U.S.A. are out of equilibrium. Since expenditure OX is greater than the value of U.K. output OA, there is a trade deficit equal to XA. (See Chapter 3.) Further, total demand for wine is now OY (by U.K.) plus

47

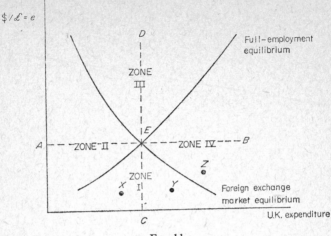

FIG. 11

NG (by U.S.) which is clearly greater than full-employment supply in the United States *AO′*.

Assuming that the U.S.A. continues to maintain its total expenditure at the same level *OA′*, we can now trace out the relationship between the exchange rate and U.K. expenditure necessary to maintain full-employment. The higher the exchange rate, the greater will be the excess supply of cloth that must be eliminated. Hence the greater must be the increase in expenditure to eliminate it. This relationship is traced out in Fig. 11, by the schedule labelled full-employment equilibrium.

Following Swan [76] we have divided Fig. 11 into four zones:

    ZONE I: over-full employment and trade surplus
    ZONE II: under-full employment and trade surplus
    ZONE III: under-full employment and trade deficit
    ZONE IV: over-full employment and trade deficit

The importance of this diagram is that it suggests that the authorities should follow policies which at first sight appear to be counter-intuitive. For example, suppose that the United Kingdom is at the position denoted by *X* in ZONE I. One would think that under these circumstances one would always want to *reduce* expenditure as well as revaluing upward.

48

However, to reach E where both goals are achieved the United Kingdom must *increase* expenditure and revalue upwards. The intuitive policy would only work in ZONE I for a position such as Y.

It is worthwhile pointing out another example: position Z. Even though the United Kingdom has a trade deficit here it must revalue its exchange rate upwards, not devalue, even though it has a trade deficit. In addition, it must also reduce total expenditure.

Often the authorities have thought it possible to achieve both internal and external balance by using only one policy instrument. However, this would indeed be an extremely fortuitous situation. It would only be possible along the dotted line DC where the exchange rate could be used to reach S and along the line AB where expenditure policy could be utilised.

The major drawback of this analysis is that it neglects what may be going on in the rest of the world. In essence it assumes that (1) the United Kingdom is sufficiently small that any disequilibria experienced in the United States can be neglected and (2) that America is following a policy designed to keep total expenditure constant.

In point of fact, such will generally not be the case and the United States will probably also be following policies designed to eliminate any disequilibria. The ultimate outcome will depend in large measure whether the two countries co-operate and jointly design an optimal strategy, in this case an exchange rate change, or whether they follow mutually contradictory policies.

It should be pointed out that this will not only be the case for policies involving exchange rate variations. Other expenditure-switching devices such as tariffs or quotas, will also be subject to these difficulties. For further discussion of these other techniques the reader is referred to Pearce [69].

THE EFFECTS OF DEVALUATION

A large number of writers have attempted to determine the conditions under which an exchange rate devaluation will lead to an improvement in the balance of trade. Unfortunately most of the literature that has emerged has very limited practical implications; instead, it has been concerned with deriving the logical implications of a number of specialised, restrictive assumptions. And because the number of alternative assumptions, implicit or explicit, is so large, the derived results are themselves difficult to compare. The basis for this discussion is the condition advanced by Lerner [45] in 1944. He argued that a devaluation would be successful in a two-country world if the sum of elasticities of demand for *imports* (rather than importables) by those two regions was less than minus one. Important amendments were soon made by Robinson [71] and Metzler [56] and a large literature began to develop. Notable are papers by Harberger [25], Negishi [66], Kemp [39], Hahn [23] and Tsiang [81]. Komiya [42] and Takayama [77] present useful comparisons of the various alternative formulations.

PEARCE'S CONTRIBUTION

However, Pearce [68, 69] has shown that previous research based on the Lerner condition has been misconceived in a number of ways.

First, it is misleading to talk about elasticities of demand or supply for imports or exports. Consider a commodity, some of which is imported and some of which is produced at home. The elasticity of demand for imports is thus a 'hodge-podge' of the elasticity of demand for the importable commodity and the elasticity of home supply. It is possible to talk of the elasticity of demand for an importable but not for imports. An elasticity of demand for imports would make sense only if none of the commodity were produced at home. Similarly an elasticity of supply of imports is a 'hodge-podge' of demand and supply elasticities in the exporting country.

The concept of an import or export demand elasticity is further clouded by the fact that in the short run, imports and exports may be affected by producer or consumer desires to add to or subtract from their inventories. Thus short-run

50

import and export demand and supply elasticities may depend on stock adjustments as well. As a result such elasticities are referred to as 'total' since they conceal within themselves considerable information about the underlying structure of the world economy. As Pearce has argued, 'such an elasticity is meaningless until its elements are specified'.

As Pearce has shown for a model similar to the one discussed in earlier chapters of this volume, the 'elasticity of demand for imports' is a complicated function not only of the elasticity of demand for importables, but also the propensity to consume importables, the elasticity of supply of importables and the rate of change of the balance of trade with respect to the terms of trade. Further, the 'elasticity of demand for imports' is not a constant, for it depends on the ratio of home consumption to the level of imports. From a practical point of view, this complexity is quite important. Negishi [66] has attempted to justify the use of 'total elasticities' on the grounds that they are easily estimated on statistical grounds. However, this cannot be the case, since the 'elasticity' itself will be a variable as noted above.

Pearce's second important contribution involved the introduction of non-traded commodities into the analysis. Since a reasonable proportion of consumer expenditure in most countries is on services, this is obviously a highly realistic assumption. Under such conditions, even if the formula indicating the effect of a devaluation is properly specified, it is impossible to determine whether that devaluation will lead to an improvement or deterioration in the balance of trade without knowledge of the *magnitudes* of the various parameters involved. Recently in conjunction with the Southampton econometric model building project, Pearce has outlined the informational requirements necessary to study the effects of a devaluation properly. For an outline of this project the reader is referred to chapter 19 of his *International Trade* [69].

8 Financial Institutions and the Foreign Exchange Market

So far we have explicitly assumed that financial relationships were either rather crude (e.g., the naïve gold-standard mechanism) or simply unimportant. If we are to make any progress toward understanding actual international monetary problems, this simplistic approach will have to be modified. In this chapter, we shall set the stage for such a development by outlining the relationship between international payments and the domestic banking system. Those readers with some familiarity with foreign exchange operations will find the analysis still relatively simple compared to the complexities of the real world. Nevertheless, as argued in Chapter 1, our procedure remains helpful since it enables us to concentrate upon certain key features of the monetary system.

There are essentially three types of operators in the foreign exchange market:

1. *The dealers*, who are banks, and operate on behalf of their customers, firms or individuals, who may want to buy or sell foreign currency. In order to meet the needs of their customers, the dealers maintain deposits with correspondent banks abroad. When a customer wants to buy foreign currency for, say, business purposes abroad, part of this deposit will be transferred to the customer. Conversely, that deposit will increase when a customer sells foreign exchange to the bank.

The transfer of foreign exchange between the customer and the bank's deposit abroad are usually arranged by cablegram.

The bank will have some idea of a desired inventory of foreign exchange that it would like to maintain over time. The size of this inventory will depend on a number of factors:

(a) The probability that customers will want to make large purchases of foreign exchange at any point of time.

(b) The profits made by the bank from commissions on such transactions.

(c) The return which the bank could make if it invested some of its funds in other assets.

2. *Brokers*, who act as intermediaries between banks. If the bank's inventory of foreign exchange rises above (falls below) the desired level, the bank may want to sell (buy) currency. The job of the broker is to act as an intermediary between one or more other banks who want to buy the foreign exchange now for sale.

3. *The central bank*, whose task, under current arrangements, is to see that a particular exchange rate is maintained. All three sets of operators are linked by a complex communications network. Thus if the Bank of England sees that the cost of pounds in terms of dollars is falling below a target rate, it can step in to buy dollars and thus support the market. Thus, much as commercial banks do, central banks will also maintain inventories of foreign exchange (or what is equivalent, gold). Gold is accepted (and often preferred) in lieu of foreign exchange at a specified price per ounce. In either case, the Bank of England will sell off its reserves to prevent the dollar price of pounds from falling below a desired level and conversely.

To understand the manner in which these institutions may interact, let us consider several examples.

Situation I

A British importer desires $240,000 in order to pay for goods ordered from a U.S. exporter. His bank arranges to transfer this amount from its own account at a correspondent in the United States to an account in the name of the British importer. The exchange rate is $2.40 per pound. The importer then writes a cheque made out to the U.S. exporter. The net result of this transaction can be illustrated by use of balance sheet accounts. For simplicity assume that the bank of the U.S. exporter and the correspondent of U.K. Bank *B* are one and the same: U.S. Bank *A* (Table I).

TABLE I

U.S. Bank *A*		U.K. Bank *B*	
Assets	Liabilities	Assets	Liabilities
	Deposit of U.S. exporter + $240,000	Deposit at correspondent in U.S. − £100,000	Deposit of U.K. importer − £100,000
	Deposit of U.K. correspondent − $240,000		

As already indicated, the British Bank maintains an account with a correspondent in the United States in order to meet the needs of customers such as the importer. Therefore unless that account with U.S. Bank *A* was abnormally high, U.K. Bank *B* will want to replenish it. There are several possibilities.

Situation II
British exporters to the United States may have received funds equivalent to $240,000 and have asked U.K. Bank *B* to

TABLE II

U.S. Bank *A*		U.K. Bank *B*	
Assets	Liabilities	Assets	Liabilities
	Deposit of U.S. importer − $240,000	Deposit at U.S. correspondent + £100,000	Deposit of U.K. exporter + £100,000
	Deposit of U.K. correspondent + $240,000		

exchange these funds for pounds. This bank will then deposit these dollars with its correspondent, so that transactions I and II taken together leave the banks' net positions unchanged (Table II).

If Tables I and II are consolidated, the reader can see that there will have been no net change in the asset or liability position of the U.S. banking system.

Situation III

The previous case would indeed be fortuitous. More likely is the situation where the U.K. exporter will exchange his dollars for pounds at a bank other than U.K. Bank *B*, say U.K. Bank *C*. If this bank now finds itself holding more dollars than it desires, it will want to sell them on the foreign exchange market. At the same time U.K. Bank *B* will want to replenish the dollars disposed of in situation I. Using their communications network the Banks may establish direct contact with each other or indirect contact through a broker, who will charge a commission for his services. Bank *C* therefore sells the dollars to Bank *B*. The latter's cash reserves will fall while the formers' will increase.

Situation IV

In situations II and III the demand and supply of foreign exchange were equal. However, there may be no private individual or firm who at the current exchange rate has dollars to sell which Bank *B* can buy to replenish its inventories of dollars. What happens in such cases will clearly depend upon the role that the monetary authorities play and the 'rules of the game' that they follow.

At one extreme, the central banks of Britain and America might have decided that the exchange rate should be rigidly fixed at $2.40 per pound. To achieve this goal, the two central banks agree to purchase any excess supply or to provide any excess demand of foreign exchange. Let us suppose that to accommodate Bank *B*'s desire to replenish its inventory of dollars, the Bank of England draws down its reserve holdings of dollars. To obtain these dollars, Bank *B* uses some of its reserves held at the Bank of England (Table III(*a*)). From the U.S.

TABLE III(a)

| U.K. Bank B | | Bank of England | |
Assets	Liabilities	Assets	Liabilities
Deposit at correspondent in U.S. +£100,000		Dollar deposit at Federal Reserve −£100,000	Reserves of Bank B −£100,000
Reserves held at Bank of England −£100,000			

point of view, Bank A will now have an additional deposit and its reserves increase accordingly (Table III(b)). On the U.S. side, we find that bank reserves have increased as a result of the increased deposit of the U.K. correspondent.

TABLE III(b)

| U.S. Bank A | | Federal Reserve | |
Assets	Liabilities	Assets	Liabilities
Reserves +$240,000	Deposit of U.K. correspondent +$240,000		Deposit of Bank of England −$240,000
			Reserves of Bank A +$240,000

The implications of this intervention are quite important. Bank reserves have increased in the United States but have decreased in the United Kingdom. This implies that unless there is some offsetting action by the central banks (say through open market operations) there will be a contraction of the money supply in the United Kingdom and an increase in the United States. Economic activity will slow down in the former country and increase in the latter. If both countries were

57

initially at full-employment, unemployment would occur in the U.K., unless wages are flexible; and inflation would arise in the U.S.

In addition to the domestic implications of the above situation, the 'international liquidity' position of both countries has been altered. In order to maintain the fixed rates, each authority must be prepared to intervene in the foreign exchange market. To do this, inventories of foreign currencies must be maintained – added to when there is an excess supply, subtracted from when there is an excess demand for foreign exchange. In the above example, the liquidity position of the Bank of England has deteriorated as a result of their intervention in the foreign exchange market when they sold dollars. Similarly the net international liquidity position of the Federal Reserve improved since a liability to the Bank of England was reduced.

Foreign currencies are not the only form of international liquidity that the monetary authorities may hold. Even though gold is no longer used as a medium of exchange in domestic market transactions, in industrial countries, most authorities

TABLE IV

| Bank of England | | Federal Reserve | |
Assets	Liabilities	Assets	Liabilities
Gold holdings −£100,000	Reserves of Bank B −£100,000	Gold holdings +$240,000	Reserves of Bank A +$240,000

do hold gold for international payments purposes. Thus, instead of using its dollar deposit, the Bank of England could draw on its holdings of gold, sell them to the Federal Reserve at a pre-specified price for dollars and then use these dollars to intervene in the foreign exchange market.

The balance sheets of the central banks would now appear as in Table IV instead of as depicted in Tables III(a) and III(b).

An interesting comparison can now be made. The impact of

central-bank intervention in the foreign exchange market is the same as that of an open market operation. Consider the case where the Bank of England sells £100,000 securities on

TABLE V

| U.K. Bank *A* | | Bank of England | |
Assets	Liabilities	Assets	Liabilities
Reserves held at the Bank of England −£100,000	Deposit of securities dealer −£100,000	Security portfolio −£100,000	Reserves of Bank *A* −£100,000

the open market (Table V). The dealer who buys the securities pays by drawing a cheque on his bank. The money supply decreases; bank reserves fall. From the Bank of England's viewpoint, this represents a decrease in its liabilities. However, this decrease exactly matches the reduction in its assets as a result of the sale of securities from its security portfolio.

THE BALANCE OF PAYMENTS

It will now be convenient to turn our attention to problems of balance-of-payments accounting and the definition of payments deficits and surpluses.

We first note the definitions of debit and credit entries that have been adopted by the International Monetary Fund [32]:

Credit entries – are made for the provision of goods and services or of financial items, whether they are sold, bartered, or furnished without a *quid pro quo*.

Debit entries – are made for the acquisition of goods and services or financial items, whether these items are purchased, obtained by barter, or acquired without a *quid pro quo*.

In addition, we shall distinguish several categories of entries:
(1) The current account – exports and imports, travel expenditures, transportation services, etc.
(2) The capital account – changes in the home assets or liabilities held by private foreigners, changes in the

59

assets or liabilities held abroad by private citizens of the home country.

(3) Official settlements or total currency flow – transactions involving the monetary authorities.

The first important point to recognise is that every transaction involves two entries in the balance-of-payments accounts. This is so because every transaction involves the exchange of one item for another. For example, consider the initial example of this chapter: U.K. imports from the United States led to the reduction in a U.K. asset held abroad. The imports are clearly a debit entry in the U.K. balance of payments whereas the decrease in foreign denominated assets is equivalent to an

TABLE VI   U.K. Balance of Payments

	Debits	Credits
I. Current account	Imports £100,000	
II. Capital account		Decrease in foreign denominated assets £100,000
III. Official settlements		

export of a financial item (Table VI). Now compare this with the case arising from situation IV where U.K. imports led to a reduction in Bank of England holdings of dollars (Table VII).

TABLE VII   U.K. Balance of Payments

	Debits	Credits
I. Current account	Imports £100,000	
II. Capital account		
III. Official settlements		Reduction in Bank of England's gold holdings £100,000

In either of these cases, the debit and credit columns will always add up to the same amount. This will also be the result for any other possible transaction. But how can there then be a balance-of-payments deficit or surplus? The answer is simply that a deficit or surplus measure depends on how we organise the accounts. It is an analytic measure whose calculation depends on what we want to show.

There are several approaches which have been adopted in the past. One approach of interest attempts to measure the excess demand or supply for foreign exchange which must be met by official intervention. In this case we would draw the line just above the official settlements entries. If the debit and credit items above this line are positive there is said to be a surplus; if they are negative, there is a deficit. Thus in Table VI, there is neither a deficit nor surplus, whereas the situation in Table VII shows a deficit.

More detailed discussion of foreign exchange operations is given in Chapter 10, where the reader should check for useful references. For additional discussion of domestic banking policies and analysis see Rowan [72] and Harrod [26]. Perhaps the best source of additional material on balance-of-payments accounting is the Bernstein Report [70]. It is there where a strong case has been made for the official settlements concept, now adopted by the United States. A similar measure, called total currency flow, is used by Great Britain. It is discussed in [8].

9 Speculation, Hedging and Arbitrage

Perhaps the most difficult problem that economists and policy makers face is understanding how the existence of uncertainty affects people's behaviour and in particular their reaction to various economic policies. In the simple model developed in earlier chapters, we emphasised that the informational requirements for the achievement of equilibrium are quite large. When we realise that people base their decisions not only on current prices and incomes but also on expectations about the future values of these variables, the magnitude of the problem becomes apparent. As a result buyers and sellers gather whatever information is readily available and form expectations about prices, etc. on the basis of this. This means that although they may often be correct, their actions may sometimes lead markets away from their equilibrium positions. The purpose of this chapter is to explain some of the transactions that arise in the foreign exchange market because of uncertainty and to show how the demand and supply of foreign exchange may be affected by changes in expectations, particularly about exchange rates. In Chapters 10 and 11 this theme will be returned to when we examine the implications of alternative exchange rate mechanisms. One conclusion will become quite clear: it is extremely difficult to reach any decision about the most desirable international monetary system without more information about the activities discussed in this chapter.

THE FORWARD MARKET

So far we have depicted the foreign exchange market as a place where currencies are bought or sold for *immediate* delivery.

However, it is possible to buy or sell foreign exchange for *future* delivery. Such contracts are usually for 30, 60 or 90 days although they may be for some other duration, possibly longer. Readers will find that most newspapers with comprehensive financial sections quote not only the current or *spot* rate between dollars and pounds but also the *forward* exchange rates for the 30, 60 and 90 days periods.

The existence of forward exchange markets facilitates four important types of transactions: (1) covering, (2) hedging (3) arbitrage and (4) speculation. All arise directly or indirectly because of uncertainty as to future rates. All have important implications for balance-of-payments adjustment. Therefore let us examine what each of these operations entails.

COVERING

Usually there is a reasonable period of time between when a contract is entered into for the sale or delivery of a product, and when the good is actually delivered and paid for. This lag may arise for a number of reasons. The buyer and seller are located some distance apart with the result that time must be taken for transportation. Or the product is not available from stock. Time must be taken to produce it.

During the period between contract and delivery, either the importer or exporter is subject to exchange risk.[1] For example, suppose a British importer agrees to pay a U.S. exporter $250 or £100 upon delivery of a certain product. The current exchange rate is $2.50 per pound sterling, and this is the rate used in the contract. If the exchange rate should fall to $2.40, the British importer would have to pay approximately £104 instead of £100. He will suffer a loss. If the rate had risen above £2.50 to say $2.60, the importer would be able to pay less than otherwise.

If the importer wanted to avoid the possibility of loss, he could cover his position by buying dollars in the forward

[1] If the contract is written in terms of a third currency, both will be subject to the risk. For example, German imports of coffee from Brazil might be paid for with U.S. dollars.

exchange market, for delivery on a date on or close to when the goods are delivered. In this way he has insured himself, i.e. he will pay the rate specified in the forward contract. His asset-liability position is now as follows. He has a liability to pay $250 to the U.S. exporter. This is exactly matched by his forward contract, an asset worth $250. If he did not cover his position he would be maintaining a short *open* position. It is short in the sense that his foreign liabilities are greater than his foreign assets. The converse would be called a long, open position.

The forward exchange market is not the only vehicle by which the importer can cover himself against exchange risk. He could borrow sufficient funds in Britain, buy dollars spot and invest them in the United States for the requisite period of time. Whether he does this or uses the forward market depend on which operation costs less. For simplicity let us suppose that the $250 are due to be paid one year from now. At the end of the year he must pay back the amount borrowed (Z) plus interest or

$$Z(1 + r_{UK}) \tag{9.1}$$

where r_{UK} is the interest rate in the U.K. at which the importer borrows. In return he receives his $250, i.e.

$$Z \cdot e_s(1 + r_{US}) = \$250 \tag{9.2}$$

where e_s is the dollar/pound spot rate and r_{US} the interest rate obtainable in the United States. If he had operated in the forward market he would have bought $250 forward for X pounds, that is

$$X \cdot e_f = \$250 \tag{9.3}$$

where e_f is the dollar/pound forward rate.

We can rearrange (9.2) to obtain an expression for Z

$$Z = \frac{\$250}{e_s(1 + r_{US})} \tag{9.4}$$

If we multiply by $(1 + r_{UK})$ we have an expression for the cost of this covering operation

$$Z(1 + r_{UK}) = \frac{\$250(1 + r_{UK})}{e_s(1 + r_{US})} \tag{9.5}$$

The cost of the forward operation is

$$X = \frac{\$250}{e_\mathrm{f}} \tag{9.6}$$

Thus if $(1+r_\mathrm{UK})/e_\mathrm{s}(1+r_\mathrm{US})$ is greater than $1/e_\mathrm{f}$ importers will prefer to cover by a forward transaction. If the inequality is reversed, they will prefer a spot transaction. If the two expressions are equal, the importers will be indifferent between the two procedures.

An interesting link between the spot and forward markets can be examined at this point. Generally the dealers who write the forward contracts will not want to maintain open positions themselves. In the above example a dealer has agreed to sell the British importer \$250 of a specified rate. If he has contracts to buy dollars in the future equivalent to \$250, the dealer is covered. However, if he does not have such contracts he will have to buy spot dollars unless he wants to maintain an open position. The implication here is that under such circumstances an increase in the demand for forward dollars may lead to an increase in demand for spot dollars.

HEDGING

In the previous section we talked about traders eliminating an open foreign exchange position when they had an asset or liability which was to be realised or paid at a specified date. Suppose, however, that an American owns a plant in the United Kingdom. This asset does not have a specified life. If there is an expectation of a British devaluation, the American owner would want to sell the asset value of his plant forward in order to involve a capital loss. This operation is called *hedging*.

ARBITRAGE

For any particular currency there may be several foreign exchange markets throughout the world. As a result exchange rates may differ from place to place. However, such differences will be only temporary. Dealers will tend to buy foreign exchange where its price is low and sell it where its price is high. This is an example of spatial arbitrage.

Of particular importance to foreign exchange markets is an operation called *covered interest rate arbitrage*. Its importance derives from the fact that it not only links the spot and forward exchange rates between two currencies but also the interest rates in the two countries involved. Let us consider the situation of a British investor with X pounds to invest. He could buy U.K. securities with a yield of r_{UK}. At the end of a year he would possess

$$X(1 + r_{UK}) \tag{9.7}$$

However, he could exchange his X pounds for U.S. dollars at the current exchange rate e_s and then invest the funds in the United States with a yield r_{US}. At the end of the year he would possess dollars equal to

$$X \cdot e_s(1 + r_{US}) \tag{9.8}$$

However, there is no guarantee that over the coming year, the exchange rate will not vary so as to make this investment unprofitable when converted back into pounds. To avoid the exchange risk he can sell the dollars forward with the result that at the end of the year he will receive pounds equal to

$$\frac{X \cdot e_s(1 + r_{US})}{e_f} \tag{9.9}$$

The latter operation is called covered interest rate arbitrage. Whether it will be undertaken or not depends on whether the expression (9.9) is greater or less than (9.7). If it is less, then investors will find it more profitable to invest in the United Kingdom.

In the short run, at least, many countries will attempt to maintain interest rates as well as the spot exchange rate fixed. The latter has been a basic rule of the International Monetary Fund (I.M.F.). Let us now suppose that it is more profitable for British investors to undertake covered interest rate arbitrage. As a result there will be an increased demand for spot dollars and an increased supply of forward dollars. Any net excess demand for dollars will be met out of official exchange reserves in order to keep the spot rate fixed. However, without any support in the forward market the price of pounds there, e_f, will rise. As a result the expression (9.9) will become smaller and smaller as funds flow from Britain to America. Eventually (9.9) and (9.7) will become equal, and at that point there will be no further incentive for covered interest rate arbitrage. This will occur when

$$(1 + r_{UK}) = \frac{e_s(1 + r_{US})}{e_f}$$

It will be noticed that this is also exactly equal to the condition when foreign traders are indifferent between forward cover and operating in the spot market.

The relationship between spot and forward exchange rates is often expressed in terms of whether or not the forward rate is at a premium or a discount in relation to the spot rate. This premium or discount can be written as a percentage of the spot rate

$$p = \frac{e_f - e_s}{e_s}$$

and in equilibrium will equal

$$\frac{r_{US} - r_{UK}}{1 + r_{UK}}$$

SPECULATION

So far our discussion has been based mainly on operations where individuals with assets or liabilities in foreign currencies have desired to avoid the risks associated with potential exchange rate variations. However, there may be individuals with such strong expectations about exchange-rate movements that they will deliberately incur an *open* position in a particular currency with a view to making a profit off the exchange-rate movement. For example, a Briton expecting a devaluation of the pound could purchase spot dollars. If the devaluation actually occurred he could then sell the dollars for more pounds than he originally possessed. Or he could operate in the forward market by selling pounds forward and then with the proceeds of the sale buying back more pounds than were originally contracted.

LEADS AND LAGS

While pure speculation can and often does play an important role in foreign exchange market activity there is another type of operation which has grown in importance. This is the problem of leads and lags and arises when importers and exporters, expecting an exchange-rate variation, undertake not only to change the timing with which payment is made for an order, but also to change the timing of the orders themselves.

Two examples will serve to illustrate the implications of leads and lags. One of the major arguments used in favour of a fixed exchange-rate system is that it encourages an atmosphere of certainty and hence stimulates trade and investment. Let us suppose that exchange rates have not been altered for a considerable period. As a result international traders may feel that there is no need to cover themselves against any adverse exchange-rate movements. However, let us now suppose that there is a widespread belief that the pound will be devalued. In these circumstances, some traders with previously uncovered positions may find it advantageous to cover. This would be true of British importers with liabilities in dollars and U.S. exporters with assets in pounds. As a result there will be a large increase in demand for both spot and forward dollars and a loss of reserves as the British authorities attempt to maintain the spot rate.

If there have been recent exchange-rate variations or indeed if the international monetary system is based on flexible rates, traders may be accustomed to covering all their transactions. However, the problem of leads and lags will still arise. Again let us suppose that there is expectation of a pound devaluation.

American importers with liabilities in pounds and British exporters with assets denominated in dollars will now find it potentially advantageous to assume open rather than covered positions. If the devaluation does occur, the former will be able to pay his debts with fewer dollars while the latter will find their dollars worth more pounds. In either case, the assumption of open positions by traders will increase the demand for dollars and again lead to a loss in British reserves.

A useful introduction to foreign exchange market activities is contained in Holmes and Schott [28]. A more comprehensive text is Einzig's [14]. Other relevant material on the relation between spot and forward markets is contained in Spraos [75] and Tsiang [80]. A discussion of official intervention in the forward market appears in [9].

10 Capital Flows and International Adjustment

As soon as we allow for international financial transactions, we can no longer treat monetary and fiscal policy as substitutes with respect to their short-run impact on output and employment. In this chapter we shall examine the implications of such capital flows between countries under fixed and flexible exchange-rate systems. The procedure adopted in most of the literature has been to modify the standard Keynesian macroeconomic model. Notable here is the work of Mundell [62]. Related articles by Johnson [35], Ingram [30, 31], McKenzie [47] and Krueger [43] are also worth the reader's attention.

ACCOUNTING RELATIONSHIPS

It is possible to measure national output Y in several ways, two of which are of interest here. On the one hand, we can calculate the value of the output itself. Or we can add up how people dispose of their incomes. For the model under consideration now, the first approach enables us to write

$$Y \equiv C + I + G + X - M$$

where C = total consumption
I = gross investment
G = government spending
X = exports
M = imports

We subtract imports since accounting custom includes imports of consumables, investment goods and government purchases abroad in C, I and G respectively. Once M is netted out, we have a measure of the value of domestic output.

These funds are then distributed in the form of wages, interest, rent and profits. And these in turn are spent on consumption, savings (S) and taxes (T). Therefore

$$Y \equiv C + S + T$$

ADJUSTMENT TO EQUILIBRIUM

As in the previous model inventory adjustments will play an important role. From an analytical point of view, gross investment I can be divided into two categories: planned (I^p) and unplanned investment (I^u). For this model, we shall assume that I^p consists of investment in plant and equipment, in residential housing and in *planned* inventory changes. On the other hand I^u consists of unplanned inventory changes. The reason why firms desire to hold inventories is that they cannot forecast exactly what demands they will face from day to day. They want to hold stocks sufficiently high that the chances are fairly remote that they will not be able to meet the needs of their customers. Yet they do not want them too high, for idle resources do not yield profits.

In the following analysis, let us start from a position where desired and actual inventories are equal. There will be many different combinations of income and interest rate which will satisfy the equilibrium condition described above. To understand this, consider the following exercise. Suppose that we are in a particular equilibrium position and that G and X are constant. Any higher level of income cannot be sustained with the given interest rate. At the higher income level, $S + T + M$ has increased as well; therefore

$$S + T + M > I^p + G + X$$

The unplanned inventory change will be positive, and as a result, there will be a tendency for output to contract. For an equilibrium to be established at the higher level of income, interest rates must be lowered so as to increase the level of

72

planned investment. In other words, the higher the level of income, the lower must be the level of interest rate in order to maintain equilibrium in the real sector. This relationship is depicted in Fig. 12 as the *XIG–MST* schedule. This schedule is simply a modification of the standard *IS* schedule developed in macro-economic theory. See Rowan [72]. Any increase in government spending (or exports) will lead to an increase in

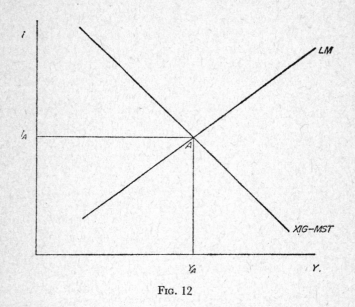

Fig. 12

output at any given interest rate and hence involves a shift to the right of the *XIG–MST* schedule. Conversely if *G* decreases.

It is important to recognise that the equilibrium condition does not necessarily require that (1) savings should equal investment, (2) government spending should equal tax receipts or (3) exports should equal imports. Two examples should establish why this is so. First, suppose that there is a zero trade balance, but that government spending is greater than tax receipts. This is compatible with equilibrium in the real sector only if saving is greater than investment by the amount of government deficit. What is happening is as follows.

73

The government is issuing securities to cover the deficit and these are being accumulated by individuals as savings. Second, suppose that savings equal investment and that there is a deficit on government account. As a result, equilibrium can only occur if imports are greater than exports. The trade deficit is being financed by the government securities being sold abroad to the extent of the government deficit. Other situations can, of course, be constructed.

Now let us examine the conditions for equilibrium in the financial sector. This occurs when the demand for and supply of money are equal. The factors affecting both money demand and supply are extremely complicated. Since there is not the opportunity to present a full discussion of these factors in a short volume, I shall restrict my discussion to a rather naive framework. First, I shall assume that the money supply can be controlled by the central bank at its discretion. Second, I shall assume that the demand for money depends on the level of income and the interest rate. The higher the level of income the greater the opportunity cost of holding idle funds. Thus the lower the demand for money.

Given this functional relationship we can now trace out in Fig. 12 the various levels of income and interest rate which will bring about equilibrium in the financial sector. Suppose that we are initially at an equilibrium point with money demand equal to supply. If income increases there will be an excess demand for funds. If, however, the interest rate increases this excess demand can be eliminated. Thus the greater the level of income, the higher must be the interest rate for equilibrium to exist in the financial sector.

There is obviously only one point, A, in Fig. 12 where the two sectors can simultaneously be in equilibrium. Let us now assume that the level of interest rate abroad is also equal to i_A and that capital is completely mobile and sensitive to any difference between home and foreign interest rates. Thus if imports are greater than exports the equilibrium condition above implies either that planned investment is greater than savings or that government spending is greater than tax receipts, or both. The trade deficit is thus covered by the sale abroad of assets to finance private investment or government spending.

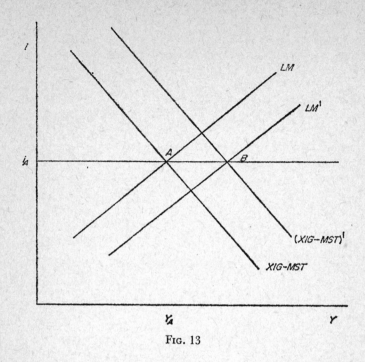

FIG. 13

FIXED EXCHANGE RATES

Now let us examine the impact of monetary and fiscal policy under a regime of fixed exchange rates. Suppose that the authorities increase government spending in order to reduce unemployment. This shifts the *XIG–MST* schedule to the right as in Fig. 13. Income rises with a consequent increase in the demand for money. As a result, there is upward pressure on interest rates; however, since capital is completely mobile between countries, funds flow in from abroad to purchase home assets. Initially this leads to surplus on capital account and an overall balance-of-payments surplus. As a result the money supply increases (Cf. Chapter 8). This in turn shifts the *LM* schedule to the right.

As income increases, the trade balance will deteriorate and gradually reduce and eliminate the overall payments surplus. The trade deficit will exactly offset the surplus on capital

75

account. This is the situation at B. Here part of the securities issued to finance the government deficit are purchased abroad and part are accumulated as private savings at home. This can be seen by rewriting the equilibrium relationship as:

$$(G-T) = (M-X) + (S-I^p)$$

Since X and I^p remain constant and both M and S increase, part of the additional securities goes to each set of investors.

The theory of capital movements in this model is quite important (it will be critically analysed at the end of the chapter). In the following analysis we assume that the country is sufficiently small to be a price taker, i.e. its actions have no effect on world prices or interest rates. These variables can be treated as given. Thus if there is excess supply for a commodity at the world price, this will be purchased by foreigners. Similarly if there is excess demand for a product, this will be satisfied through imports from abroad.

Exactly the same logic is applied in this model to the analysis of capital flows. Suppose that at the world level of interest rates, there exists an excess supply of securities. If there were controls preventing capital movements, interest rates would tend to rise at home. However, we assume perfect mobility of capital, and as a result the excess supply is purchased by foreigners.

Fiscal policy thus has the desired effect of increasing output and employment. This, however, is not true with respect to monetary policy. Suppose the money supply is increased. This shifts the LM schedule to the right. There is now an excess supply of money and downward pressure on interest rates. But this causes a capital outflow. The supply of pounds on the foreign exchange market is greater than the demand. The authorities intervene to buy up the excess (again, in order to keep the exchange rate constant) with the result that the money supply decreases. The LM schedule shifts back to its original position. Monetary policy is ineffective.

The central bank could continue to buy securities in an attempt to keep the LM schedule shifted out. But this will mean a continual payments deficit and loss of gold or foreign exchange reserves. Since the latter is not in unlimited supply the authorities must at some point abandon this policy. Faced with this constraint, they have frequently resorted to various sorts of capital controls. While in reality capital flows may not be completely responsive to interest rate differentials the responsiveness is liable to be great enough to cause problems. By instituting controls the responsiveness can be reduced even further. For example, during periods of restrictive monetary policy, limits could be placed on banks' net foreign lending, or higher reserve requirements might be made against deposits by foreigners. A detailed list of various controls has been presented by the O.E.C.D. [67].

FLEXIBLE EXCHANGE RATES

Under a system of flexible exchange rates, monetary policy is effective whereas fiscal policy is not. Let us suppose that the authorities undertake to reduce unemployment by increasing the level of government spending. This will shift the $XIG–MST$ schedule to the right, as before, and will tend to increase interest rates. See Fig. 14. This will occur since (a) bonds have been

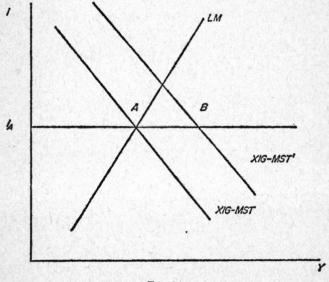

Fig. 14

issued to finance some of the additional government expenditure and (*b*) income has increased, with the result that the transactions demand for money is now larger. The higher interest rates will cause a capital inflow. However, instead of leading to an increase in cash balances as under a fixed exchange rate system, the inflow will cause an appreciation in the exchange rate. Provided that all elasticities and propensities are of the 'right' magnitude, foreign produce will be substituted for home produced goods, causing the *XIG–MST* schedule to shift back to its original position. There is a deterioration in the trade balance which just offsets the surplus on capital account. The interest rate must return to the world level, according to the maintained theory, or the capital flow will continue to increase. Although the level of government spending remains at its new increased level, production for export and home consumption has fallen by a corresponding amount. Fiscal policy would appear to have no impact under a flexible exchange rate system.

However, the effect of monetary policy is different. An increase in the money supply shifts the *LM* schedule to the right, thereby causing downward pressure on interest rates. There is thus a capital outflow which causes the exchange rate to depreciate. Exports increase, imports fall and home production is stimulated. This causes the *XIG–MST* schedule to shift to the right as well. A trade surplus offsets the deficit on capital account. Again the world interest rate level must be restored otherwise there will be a growing capital account deficit, leading to a further depreciation and rightward shift in the *XIG–MST* schedule. The important thing in this case is that the shift in the *XIG–MST* schedule reinforces the original shift in the *LM* schedule. The situation is the same as depicted in Fig. 13, although the process of adjustment is decidedly different.

SOME CRITICISMS

The basic problem posed by this framework is one inherent in all Keynesian type macro-models: it contains an incomplete description of the adjustment process. For example, in the above examples, when government spending increased, the actual level of inventories fell below the desired level, i.e. undesired inventory change was negative. In response output increased until such time as excess market demand was eliminated. However, we have not taken into account the fact that the actual level of inventories are still below desired inventories. Excess market demand was eliminated; however, we have neglected the additional demand on the part of business to replenish stocks. As a result the analysis must be considered only partial: the rebuilding of the stock of inventories is bound to affect the level of output and/or prices. One could argue that in the short run businesses may be passive about their inventory stocks. Yet this does not seem consistent with decisions to change output and employment: a reaction indicating that businesses are not adopting a passive attitude.

There is another important way in which the analysis does not properly account for stock variables. In our example where government spending was increased under a fixed exchange rate system, we found that part of the issue of government securities was accumulated by home investors as savings and part was sold abroad and covered the trade deficit. Presumably, however, individuals at home as well as abroad will have some idea of the desired stock of securities that they wish to hold at given interest rates and income levels. And when this desired stock is achieved they will no longer be willing to accumulate additional securities. Obviously we need to reformulate the above analysis in terms of portfolio adjustment theory. Unfortunately attempts along these lines are still very rudimentary. However, notable is the work of McKinnon and Oates [49] and McKinnon [50] who examine the implications of capital movements within a simple portfolio adjustment model.

Finally, it should be noted that when we discussed the flexible exchange-rate system, we assumed that exchange-rate variations had no impact on capital flows. However, even in the short run, there is bound to be some relationship. First, exchange-rate changes will lead to changes in the value of an investor's net asset position abroad. This may lead him to take capital gains (or absorb losses, whichever it may be) and to reallocate his portfolio. Second, expectations of future exchange-rate changes may cause individuals to be unresponsive to higher interest rates abroad. This would be the case if the foreign currency was expected to depreciate in value.

These comments indicate various ways in which the theory needs to be expanded if it is to be of greater practical relevance. The underlying ideas and results of the model described in this chapter nevertheless remain important, for they draw our attention to the sort of difficulties likely to arise in the short run when capital is freely mobile between countries.

11 International Monetary Reform

In the previous chapters, we have emphasised that international monetary theory, like other areas of macro-economic analysis, has been dominated by two conceptions of the adjustment process: the 'price-adjustment' and the 'inventory-adjustment' mechanisms. These are frequently referred to as Marshallian and Keynesian, respectively. We now turn our attention to the implications of these assumptions for the choice of international monetary system. In doing so, we shall be concerned with four alternatives: (1) the adjustable peg system, currently in operation; (2) a flexible exchange-rate system; (3) a common-currency arrangement: and (4) modifications of (1) and (2) which involve some flexibility.

In order to provide a background for the discussion, it is useful to note a distinction that has been drawn by monetary economists between *inside* and *outside* lags. The inside lag is the period between the time an action is needed and the time action is actually taken. Smith and Teigen [74] have further divided this span into a recognition lag – the time it takes to realise that there is a problem – and an administrative lag – the time it takes to put a particular policy in operation. Numerous discretionary policies have been discussed in previous chapters: devaluation, monetary and fiscal policies, trade policies, etc. Unfortunately it is impossible to make any general statements about the length of the inside lag, since it is bound to vary from country to country. On the one hand the recognition lag clearly depends on the quality and quantity of research activities that the authorities carry out. The administrative lag depends on the flexibility delegated to those responsible for a particular policy, e.g. trade policy, and their willingness to co-ordinate with other branches of the government. The point to note here is that the authorities face the same problem that the private sector does: the existence of uncertainty. And as a result, it is also liable to error. This problem is compounded by the fact that there are many national authorities who, unless they co-ordinate their activities, may institute mutually contradictory policies, a possibility noted in Chapter 7.

Our main concern in this chapter is with an examination of the outside lags – the period of time between when an action is taken and when its effects are felt – implied by alternative international monetary systems. Disagreements about the nature of this lag, I maintain, are at the heart of the debate about which alternative system is the 'best'. As I have argued several times throughout this volume, if we possessed complete information, there would be no problem. However, such is not the case. People act on the basis of what they believe or expect to be true about the world. Therefore they are prone to mistakes and, as a result, costs are imposed either upon themselves or upon other transactors with whom they have direct or indirect contact. Thus it is important to determine whether an international monetary system can be conceived which will minimise the costs associated with such error-formation. Unfortunately the problem is not clear cut, for while we might be able to conceive of policies designed to 'hasten equilibrium' in one market, e.g. the labour market, that same policy may promote disequilibrium in another. This problem should be apparent from the earlier discussion in Chapters 7 and 10.

FLEXIBLE EXCHANGE RATES

As we noted earlier, the Keynesian macro-economic model assumes that commodity prices remain constant in the short run. Therefore it may seem surprising that Keynes also favoured flexible exchanges. However, the two positions are completely compatible. If domestic prices do not adjust quickly when expenditure is reduced in order to eliminate a balance-of-payments deficit, then unemployment will emerge.

On the other hand if expenditure policies, in particular fiscal policy, is utilised to achieve full-employment in the short run, then the exchange rate can be allowed to vary so as to achieve external balance. The implication is that government intervention need occur only when it appears that markets are not working in the desired fashion.

Friedman [18] has argued persuasively that indeed the foreign exchange market will act in a smooth and stable fashion. He assumes that operators in the market, be they speculators or traders are 'rational'. That is, they are reasonably omniscient about future exchange-rate movements.

Let us suppose that the actual dollar/pound exchange rate is higher than that which market forces in the future will dictate. Friedman argues that operators, being smart, will foresee this event and become net purchasers of dollars. This action moves the exchange rate in the 'correct' direction.

Consider another case, when the dollar/pound rate has *temporarily* fallen below the long-run equilibrium rate. Here Friedman would argue that operators, recognising the situation, would become net purchasers of pounds and in the process would bid up the exchange rate. Thus for the system to work in either case, actual and expected changes would have to coincide. This is exactly the condition we noted earlier in Chapter 4.

However, there is no particular reason why speculators and traders should be so omniscient. There may be situations where they believe that the rate should fall, when underlying real factors call for an increase. In the long run, the error may be recognised, but in the short run the response to a false signal could set up undesirable fluctuations.

Friedman has argued that since speculators make profits, they must be correct. However, in rebuttal Baumol [3] has argued that speculation as a whole could be unprofitable if there were two groups of operators. One group, well-informed, could make large profits at the expense of a floating group of speculators who based their opinions on false data or misleading grounds. The impact of this discussion is bound to be limited by the fact that banks are unlikely to make funds readily available for speculative purposes.

Rather, destabilising patterns are more likely to arise from the leading and lagging activities of traders. For example it may be the case that importers or exporters do not normally hedge. However, if there should develop a general expectation of an adverse exchange-rate movement, many may rush to hedge their open positions. For example importers expecting a depreciation of the pound would rush to cover any assets denominated in dollars. The result would be large downward pressure on the pound. But the expectations which gave rise to this activity could be completely false and unfounded.

With respect to the operation of labour markets the implications of a flexible exchange-rate system are difficult to assess. If the exchange-rate variation is slow over time, then we can expect resources to move gradually out of industries whose market is deteriorating and into industries where demand is growing. However, if exchange-rate fluctuations are sharp then an industry which finds the price of its product abroad suddenly higher may be forced to cut back output and unemployment. This phenomena could be nationwide, affecting just a few industries, or it could be regional. If such dislocations were to be avoided, then the authorities would have to resort to very specific rather than general stabilisation policies, e.g. regional or industry-specific subsidisation. A flexible exchange-rate system does not enable a country to isolate itself from events abroad. Rather it enables the authorities to concentrate on domestic stabilisation. From a political standpoint there is a loss of sovereignty, since the authorities must respond to exchange-rate changes in order to achieve full-employment at home. That exchange-rate variation may have been indirectly generated by the actions of the authorities abroad in their attempts at stabilisation.

In order to dampen fears about potentially destabilising activity, a system of limited exchange-rate flexibility could be adopted. For example such an arrangement might allow for discretionary exchange-rate variations of, say, one-quarter of one per cent in either direction during any particular time period, perhaps a month. This would have the advantage of allowing rates to vary so as to correct imbalances. Exchange reserves would still have to be maintained, however, to prevent the rate from moving outside the pre-specified bounds.

THE ADJUSTABLE PEG SYSTEM

Under current arrangements countries maintain exchange rates fixed for prolonged periods of time. However, with the permission of the I.M.F. adjustments may be made. Under this system the problem usually arises when a country has had a long string of deficits or surpluses. Some event occurs that makes it obvious to everyone that an exchange-rate change is likely. As a result speculation and leads and lags cause even greater pressure on the currency. In the deficit country reserves fall even further; in the surplus country there is a vast inflow of funds. And all of this occurs within a short span of time. Under such conditions there is only a small chance that operators in the foreign exchange market will be incorrect. Their actions merely bring forward the day when the authorities must alter the exchange rate.

There are several difficulties with the operation of this system. First, the burden of a large relative price change is felt within a very short time-period. Depending upon how elastic demand is at home and abroad, significant resource shifts might occur, with the inevitable regional or industry short-run unemployment problems. Because of the sudden large change in the exchange rate, it appears that this difficulty is much more likely to occur under this system than under a more flexible exchange-rate arrangement.

Second, under the adjustable peg system, forward exchange facilities have not been developed sufficiently to handle the burden in periods of uncertainty. Since exchange rates are fixed for prolonged periods of time speculation, hedging or covering provide only a small volume of overall activity. However, when a crisis develops increased demands are placed on these facilities, demands which they cannot bear. One result is that covered interest rate arbitrage does not act to bring the spot and forward rates into line with international interest rate differentials. There are numerous reasons why this may occur: (1) legal or institutional obstacles to the international movement of funds; (2) the lack of suitable short-term securities; and (3) arbitrageurs may not have sufficiently large funds to commit to this operation.

The result is that the forward market breaks down just when it is needed most. Traders and other operators in the market find it extremely expensive to hedge or cover just at the time when they need to the most. The virtue of the system is that it is supposed to engender a feeling of certainty and thus promote the growth of international trade and investment. Unfortunately, in many instances, the security is liable to be quite false.

Under the adjustable peg system, there is a small degree of flexibility. Spot exchange rates may vary by one per cent either side of the peg. Halm [24] has suggested that this band of flexibility might be widened, although the basic idea of a fixed peg would be retained. From a short-run standpoint this proposal has much to offer. It enables the price mechanism to play a more important role in the adjustment process and thus may reduce pressure on a country's international liquidity position. Further, uncertainty as to which way the exchange rate is going to move within the band may tend to discourage undesirable speculative activities. On the other hand a potential problem may exist in the long run. If the exchange rate is always near one edge of the band and there has been a continuous change in its reserve position, it will be apparent to speculators which way the rate should move. When the peg is changed they will then gain at the expense of others who must adjust their activities in response to the potentially large change in the terms of trade.

COMMON CURRENCY SYSTEM

A system whereby national currencies would be abandoned and replaced by a single common unit of exchange has been proposed by the E.E.C. Quite simply, such a system represents a complete inversion of Keynes' views. First of all it represents the maximum of distrust in the ability of the foreign exchange market to achieve balance-of-payments adjustment. Instead it calls for a system much like the one operating in the United States with respect to the thirteen federal reserve districts or in the United Kingdom between England, Wales, Scotland or Northern Ireland. Since transactors all use the same currency, there is no balance-of-payments problem. In our accounting terminology, all entries appear 'above the line'.

The major benefit of such a system is that it would eliminate the uncertainty about exchange rates that is inherent in the previous two systems. As such it will tend to promote a more rapid growth in international trade and investment. However, there are potential problems involved in the use of short-run domestic stabilisation policies. As we have seen, the effectiveness of monetary policy within a region is considerably weakened under a fixed exchange-rate system, a common currency system being but an extreme example. Therefore regional monetary policies will have to be abandoned under such an arrangement and a supranational monetary authority established. This body would then set the overall monetary policy for the entire currency area. However, it is always possible that regional unemployment or inflation may emerge. In such circumstances, a policy which does not discriminate between regions may be undesirable. For example suppose that demand shifts away from the products of region A to those of region B, where both regions are initially at full-employment. As a result there will be inflation in B, and if prices are inflexible downwards in A, unemployment will emerge there. An expansionary monetary or fiscal policy will reduce unemployment but at the expense of even greater inflation in region B. An overall restrictive policy would reduce the inflation, but at the cost of even greater unemployment in A. A similar problem would emerge if technological advances occurred in one region but not in the other.

There is no straightforward way out of this dilemma, basically because the answer is a political one. A decision as to which group of people are to gain and which are to lose must be made. Obviously, the people in region B will be best off if a restrictive policy is followed: they will be fully employed with little or no increase in the cost of their purchases. Workers in A, however, will be best off if an expansionary policy is followed. Although the cost of their purchases will have increased, they will indeed all have work.

If the authorities follow a rule that everyone whether in A or B should be treated equally, then the expansionary policy will be followed: all citizens will be employed and all will face the same increase in the cost of living. The implication of this policy is that some inflation may be necessary in order to achieve full-employment under a common currency system. An alternative is that the authorities should follow regional fiscal policies. In our example this would involve higher taxes or less government spending in B and lower taxes or more government spending in A. While this would, in principle, enable full-employment to be achieved without inflation, there has been a redistribution of income away from B's citizens to those in A. The political element cannot be avoided.

A MIDDLE GROUND

On the basis of the above discussion, it is impossible to reach any general qualitative conclusions about the superiority of any one of the above systems. Each has strengths and each has weaknesses. One approach to solving this dilemma is to design an international monetary system which combines the strengths but minimises the weaknesses of the various approaches. Two such proposals, both different, will be discussed here: the formation of optimum currency areas, and the 'crawling-peg' or 'sliding-parity' proposal.

Optimum currency areas

In our discussion of the common currency proposal, we noted that a potential problem could be the emergence of regional unemployment or regional inflation. Mundell [60] has suggested that a solution to this would be to define regions within which labour is reasonably mobile. Such an 'optimum' region would have its own currency. The exchange rate between the regions would be flexible.

Mundell himself argues the difficulties with such an approach.

First of all, it would involve the re-alignment and breaking up of existing nation states – something that would be politically unacceptable. Second, it would probably involve the creation of fairly small currency areas, since the costs associated with moving great distances are fairly large for workers. In addition McKinnon [48] has argued that labour mobility may not be the only criteria for defining a region. Rather, ease of achieving international payments equilibrium and a stable price level may also be important considerations. For example an area based on a few industries may find itself subject to undue price fluctuations and income variations given cyclical changes in demand in other regions.

The crawling peg

Such a system would allow the parity to be altered fairly frequently by small amounts. It has been advocated by a number of economists including: Meade [53], Williamson [84], Murphy [64] and McKenzie [47]. In the version suggested by Meade, the authorities would be allowed to change the parity by one-sixth of one per cent in any month. Thus the maximum that it could be varied within a year would be two per cent. The aim of such a scheme is to allow the price mechanism to do some of the work in restoring balance in international payments. In doing so, it would appear to offer the monetary authorities greater control over domestic activity. At the same time, it is argued, it will tend to damp down the speculative activities that have plagued the current adjustable peg system. By allowing the exchange rate greater flexibility the authorities will increase the uncertainty as to which direction the rate is going to move. In addition, by spreading the exchange-rate adjustments over time, the costs of adjustment associated with the re-allocation of resources domestically can be more easily absorbed.

Its main weakness is the weakness of the other, alternative international monetary systems. They do not easily accommodate themselves to large, unforeseen changes either in the underlying structure of the world economy or in expectations. Furth [20] has argued that in such circumstances, speculators will know which way the rate will move and will act accordingly. Since exchange-rate movements will be constrained, the authorities will sustain large losses of reserves. However, this would also be the case under the adjustable peg. Under a purely flexible system, large changes in relative prices would have to be absorbed. The crawling peg thus appears to be a compromise solution. Further, if necessary, there is nothing to prevent the participants in such a system from agreeing to larger exchange-rate variations than those possible within the crawling-peg framework.

Bibliography

[1] J. Airov, 'The Construction of Interregional Business Cycle Models', *Journal of Regional Science*, No. 1 (1963).

[2] S. S. Alexander, 'Effects of a Devaluation on a Trade Balance', *International Monetary Fund Staff Papers* (April 1952). Reprinted in Caves and Johnson [7].

[3] W. Baumol, 'Speculation, Profitability and Stability', *Review of Economics and Statistics* (August 1957).

[4] C. F. Bickerdike, 'Instability of Foreign Exchange', *Economic Journal* (March 1920).

[5] D. W. Bushaw and R. W. Clower, *Introduction to Mathematical Economics* (Richard D. Irwin, Homewood, Ill., 1957).

[6] R. Caves, 'Flexible Exchange Rates', *American Economic Review* (May 1963).

[7] R. Caves and H. Johnson (eds.), *Readings in International Economics* (Richard D. Irwin, Homewood, Ill., 1968).

[8] Central Statistical Office, *United Kingdom Balance of Payments* (London, 1970).

[9] E. Chalmers (ed.) *Forward Exchange Intervention* (Hutchinson, 1971).

[10] J. Chipman, 'The Multi-Sector Multiplier', *Econometrica* (October 1950).

[11] R. N. Cooper, *International Finance* (Penguin, Harmondsworth, 1969).

[12] W. M. Corden, 'The Geometric Representation of Policies to Attain Internal and External Balance', *Review of Economic Studies* (October 1960). Reprinted in Cooper [11].

[13] W. M. Corden, *Recent Developments in the Theory of International Trade*, Special Papers in International Economics, No. 7 (Princeton University, International Finance Section, 1965).

[14] P. Einzig, *A Textbook on Foreign Exchange* (Macmillan, 1966).

[15] P. Einzig, *Leads and Lags* (Macmillan, 1968).

[16] H. S. Ellis and L. A. Metzler (eds.), *Readings in the Theory of International Trade* (Blakiston, Philadelphia, 1950).

[17] W. Fellner, 'On Limited Exchange-Rate Flexibility', in Fellner *et al.*, *Maintaining and Restoring Balance in International Payments* (Princeton University Press, 1966). Reprinted in Cooper [11].

[18] M. Friedman, 'The Case for Flexible Exchange Rates', in his *Essays in Positive Economics* (University of Chicago Press, 1953).

[19] M. Friedman, 'The Quantity Theory of Money – A Restatement', in his *Studies in the Quantity Theory of Money* (University of Chicago Press, 1956).

[20] J. H. Furth, 'International Monetary Reform and the "Crawling Peg" – Comment', *Review* of the Federal Reserve Bank of St Louis (July 1969).

[21] R. Goodwin, 'The Multiplier as Matrix', *Economic Journal* (December 1949).

[22] G. Haberler, *A Survey of International Trade Theory,* revised edition, Special Papers in International Economics, No. 1 (Princeton University, International Finance Section, 1961).

[23] F. H. Hahn, 'The Balance of Payments in a Monetary Economy', *Review of Economic Studies* (February 1959).

[24] G. N. Halm, *The 'Band' Proposal: The Limits of Permissible Exchange Rates Variations* (Princeton University, International Finance Section, 1965).

[25] A. Harberger, 'Currency Depreciation, Income and the Balance of Trade', *Journal of Political Economy* (February 1950). Reprinted in Caves and Johnson [7].

[26] R. Harrod, *Money* (Macmillan, 1969).

[27] J. R. Hicks, *Capital and Growth* (Oxford University Press, 1965).

[28] A. Holmes and F. Schott, *The New York Foreign Exchange Market* (Federal Reserve Bank of New York, 1965).

[29] D. Hume, 'Of The Balance of Trade', *Essays, Moral,*

Political and Literary, vol. 1 (Longmans, Green, 1898) reprinted in Cooper [11].

[30] J. Ingram, 'State and Regional Payments Mechanisms', *Quarterly Journal of Economics* (November 1959).

[31] J. Ingram, 'Some Implications of Puerto Rican Experience', in his *Regional Payments Mechanism: The Case of Puerto Rico* (University of North Carolina Press, Chapel Hill, 1962).

[32] International Monetary Fund, *Balance of Payments Manual* (Washington, D.C., 1961).

[33] H. G. Johnson, 'The Taxonomic Approach to Economic Policy', *Economic Journal* (December 1951).

[34] H. G. Johnson, 'A Simplification of Multi-country Multiplier Theory', *Canadian Journal of Economics and Politics* (May 1956).

[35] H. G. Johnson, 'Theoretical Problems of the International Monetary System', *Pakistan Development Review* (Spring 1967). Reprinted in Cooper [11].

[36] H. G. Johnson, 'The Case for Flexible Exchange Rates, 1969', in Johnson and J. Nash, *UK and Floating Exchanges* (Institute of Economic Affairs, 1969).

[37] H. G. Johnson, 'Towards a General Theory of the Balance of Payments', in *International Trade and Economic Growth* (Allen & Unwin, 1958).

[38] H. G. Johnson, 'The Monetary Approach to Balance-of-Payments Theory', in M. Connolly and A. Swoboda, *International Trade and Money* (Allen & Unwin, 1973).

[39] M. C. Kemp, *The Pure Theory of International Trade* (Prentice-Hall, Englewood Cliffs, N.J., 1969).

[40] J. M. Keynes, *The General Theory* (Macmillan, 1936).

[41] C. Kindleberger, 'Flexible Exchange Rates', in his *Europe and the Dollar* (The M.I.T. Press, Cambridge, Mass., 1966).

[42] R. Komiya, 'Monetary Assumptions, Currency Depreciation and the Balance of Trade', *The Economic Studies Quarterly* (December 1966).

[43] A. O. Krueger, 'The Impact of Alternative Government Policies under Varying Exchange Systems', *Quarterly Journal of Economics* (May 1965).

[44] A. O. Krueger, 'Balance-of-Payments Theory', *Journal of Economic Literature* (March 1969).

[45] A. P. Lerner, *The Economics of Control* (Macmillan, New York, 1944).

[46] F. Machlup, *International Trade and the National Income Multiplier* (Blakiston, Philadelphia, 1943)

[47] G. McKenzie, 'International Monetary Reform and the "Crawling Peg"', *Review* of the Federal Reserve Bank of St Louis (February 1969).

[48] R. I. McKinnon, 'Optimum Currency Areas', *American Economic Review* (September 1963). Reprinted in Cooper [11].

[49] R. McKinnon and W. Oates, *The Implications of International Economic Integration for Monetary, Fiscal and Exchange-Rate Policy,* Studies in International Finance, No. 16 (Princeton University, International Finance Section, 1966).

[50] R. McKinnon, 'Portfolio Balance and International Payments Adjustment' in R. Mundell and A. Swoboda, *Monetary Problems of the International Economy* (University of Chicago Press, 1969).

[51] A. Marshall, *The Pure Theory of Foreign Trade* (London School of Economics and Political Science, 1930) reprinted with *The Pure Theory of Domestic Values.*

[52] J. Meade, *The Balance of Payments,* vol. I of *The Theory of International Economic Policy* (Oxford University Press, 1951).

[53] J. Meade, 'The Case for Flexible Exchange Rates', *Three Banks Review* (September 1955).

[54] J. E. Meade, *A Geometry of International Trade* (Allen & Unwin, 1961).

[55] J. E. Meade, 'The International Monetary Mechanism', *The Three Banks Review* (September 1964).

[56] L. A. Metzler, 'The Theory of International Trade', in *A Survey of Contemporary Economics,* ed. H. S. Ellis, vol. I (Richard D. Irwin, Homewood, Ill., 1948).

[57] L. A. Metzler, 'A Multiple-Region Theory of Income and Trade', *Econometrica* (October 1950).

[58] L. A. Metzler, 'The Process of International Adjustment

under Conditions of Full Employment: A Keynesian View', in Caves and Johnson [7].

[59] J. S. Mill, *Principles of Political Economy* (London: Parker, 1857).

[60] R. A. Mundell, 'The Theory of Optimum Currency Areas', *American Economic Review* (November 1961).

[61] R. A. Mundell, 'The Appropriate Use of Monetary and Fiscal Policy for Internal and External Stability', *I.M.F. Staff Papers* (March 1962).

[62] R. A. Mundell, 'Capital Mobility and Stabilization Under Fixed and Flexible Exchange Rates', *Canadian Journal of Economics and Political Science* (November 1963). Reprinted in Caves and Johnson [7].

[63] R. A. Mundell, 'Hicksian Stability, Currency Markets, and the Theory of Economic Policy', in *Value Capital, and Growth*, Papers in honour of Sir John Hicks, ed. J. N. Wolfe (Edinburgh University Press, 1968).

[64] J. C. Murphy, 'Moderated Exchange Rate Variability', *National Banking Review* (December 1965).

[65] E. Nagel, 'Assumptions in Economic Theory', *American Economic Review* (May 1963).

[66] T. Negishi, 'Approaches to the Analysis of Devaluation', *International Economic Review* (June 1968).

[67] O.E.C.D., 'Controls on Capital Flows', *Economic Outlook* (December 1972).

[68] I. F. Pearce, 'The Problem of the Balance of Payments', *International Economic Review* (January 1961).

[69] I. F. Pearce, *International Trade*, Books i and ii (Macmillan 1970).

[70] Review Committee for Balance of Payments Statistics to the Bureau of the Budget, *The Balance of Payments Statistics of the United States* (U.S. Government Printing Office, Washington, D.C., 1965).

[71] J. Robinson, 'The Foreign Exchanges', in her *Essays in the Theory of Employment* (Basil Blackwell, Oxford, 1947).

[72] D. C. Rowan, *Output, Inflation and Growth* (Macmillan, 1968).

[73] J. Rueff, *Balance of Payments* (Macmillan, New York, 1967).

[74] W. L. Smith and R. L. Teigen, *Readings in Money,*

National Income and Stabilization Policy (Richard D. Irwin, Homewood, Ill., 1965).

[75] J. Spraos, 'The Theory of Forward Exchange and Recent Practice', *Manchester School* (May 1953).

[76] T. Swan, 'Long-Run Problems of the Balance of Payments', in *The Australian Economy*, ed. H. Arndt and W. M. Corden (Cheshire, Melbourne, 1963). Reprinted in Caves and Johnson [7].

[77] A. Takayama, *International Trade* (Holt, Rinehart & Winston, New York, 1972).

[78] F. Taussig, *International Trade* (Macmillan, New York, 1927).

[79] J. Tinbergen, *Economic Policy: Principles and Design*, (North-Holland, Amsterdam: 1956).

[80] S. C. Tsiang, 'The Theory of Forward Exchanges and Effects of Government Intervention on the Forward Exchange Market', *I.M.F. Staff Papers* (April 1959).

[81] S. C. Tsiang, 'The Role of Money in Trade-Balance Stability: Synthesis of the Elasticity and Absorption Approaches', *American Economic Review* (December 1961). Reprinted in Caves and Johnson [7].

[82] J. Viner, *Studies in the Theory of International Trade* (Harper, New York, 1937).

[83] J. Vanek, *International Trade: Theory and Economic Policy*, (Richard D. Irwin, Homewood, Ill., 1962).

[84] J. H. Williamson, *The Crawling Peg*, Princeton Essays in International Finance (December 1965).